Nehemiah:
A Labor of Love

Dr. Bo Wagner

Word of His Mouth Publishers
Mooresboro, NC

ISBN: 978-0-9856042-7-1
Printed in the United States of America
©2013 Dr. Bo Wagner (Robert Arthur Wagner)

Word of His Mouth Publishers
PO Box 256
Mooresboro, NC 28114
704-477-5439
www.wordofhismouth.com

Table of Content

Dedication

Nehemiah had a book named after him. Was it because he rebuilt the walls of Jerusalem? No. Nehemiah did not rebuild the walls; Nehemiah got under a burden for the walls to be rebuilt. But in order for the task to be done, he had to enlist the help of a lot of men. These men, whose names do not grace the cover of the book, made Nehemiah's dream a reality.

I understand how blessed Nehemiah was.

This book is affectionately dedicated to my wall builders, the men of the Cornerstone Baptist Church. They are many, and they are one and all a blessing! Chip Nuhrah, with me since the very first day; teacher, treasurer, song leader, respected by all. Don Robbins, builder, shouter, encourager, head of our nursing home ministry. Chuck Worley, a source of quiet strength. Jimmy Davis, one of my dearest friends, a man that defines loyalty, and yet Bruce Lee to my Chuck Norris! Tony Sutton and Brian Searcy, my tech gurus. Robert Bridges, digging in the dirt and in the Word, best concrete man in the state. Mike Drewery, church mechanic and grill master, a man who always seems to know when something needs to be done and then does it, whatever "it" is! Paul Cash, head of security, trip organizer, steady as a rock. Buck Cobb, a man that can be counted on and one of my dearest friends. Jason Porter, quietly doing right. Dave Keener, big man, big heart. Joe Keener and Ron Wheat, the best deacons a pastor ever had. Greg Potter, does not say much, but makes it count when he does. Bobby Kramer, marine, Christian, proficient at both. Ron Love, if ever a man had the pastor's back, he does. Greg McKinney, a man that has since day one been as steady as a rock. Daniel Greene, we go way back, and I am looking forward to keeping going with him way into the future. Matt Rowland, golden voice, heart for God, we needed a choir leader, and God sent us the best. John Buff, saved recently and learning at an amazing pace. Curtis Hamilton, always a smile to give, always. James Henderson, a strong right hand to me, quite literally a wall builder. Don Sessions, every pastor's dream, a man that makes sure God's man is well taken care of. Weston Bridges, up and coming yet absolutely down to earth. Josh Drewery, strong, yet tender hearted. John Fitch, who can always be counted on for an "amen!" Tony Holt, maybe the best witnesser I have ever seen. If you get near him, you *are* getting a gospel tract. Carl Ebert, maybe the most dedicated father I have ever seen. Jeff Brown, a man with a good testimony. Ted Burr, a man of depth and faithfulness. Mark Ferguson, a man who sets an example by truly loving his family. Leroy Griffin, an old friend come home. Jack Strickland, our heating and air man, steady as a rock, and always a smile no matter what he is going through. Randall Blakley, a man willing to learn and grow. James Wood, who has recently become the absolute definition of II Corinthians 5:17. Kenneth Mull, one of the most unexpected friends I have ever had, and one that I thank God for pretty much every day. Sterling Cole, a young man that I appreciate. Gordon Heisler, one of my silver-haired saints, faithful here for a very long time. Larry Laws, got saved here not too long ago and has the changed life to prove it!

These men are the best. They run the nursing home ministry and have grown it from two church members being there for it to twenty-five church members being there for it and that many residents too! They witness, they work, they pray, they tithe, they keep things running whenever I am gone in revival, they sing, they praise, they back me up, they are amazing.

I realize that any of these men are capable of falling or of falling out with me. But I hope none of them ever do, because all of them mean the world to me.

These men are my friends.

Introduction

In 722 B.C., after years of disobedience, the Northern Kingdom of Israel fell captive to Assyria. But the Southern Kingdom of Judah continued on for another 136 years with a mixture of good kings and bad kings. All the while, though, she kept repeating the same mistakes the Northern Kingdom had made, following after idols instead of the one true God. Finally, the patience of God ran out, and He commissioned the Chaldeans, headed by the great city of Babylon and the mighty King Nebuchadnezzar, to come against His people.

In the lead-up to that event, God called a man named Jeremiah, the son of Hilkiah of the priests in Anathoth, to prophesy against Judah. Jeremiah was to tell them that their time had run out. God was sending the armies of the North against them, and they were going to go into captivity for seventy years.

Judah rebelled against the message. They even had their favorite false prophet, Zedekiah, tell everyone that Jeremiah was lying and that Judah would defeat the Babylonians. Everyone found out pretty quickly, the hard way, that Zedekiah was wrong and Jeremiah was right. After a lengthy siege, Jerusalem fell to Babylon in 586 B.C. When they fell, King Nebuchadnezzar commanded his men to take many of the children and grandchildren of the princes of the land and also many other nobles and leaders and bring them into captivity, just as God had prophesied. Some of them have names that are familiar to you: Daniel, Shadrach, Meshach, Abednego. But many thousands more were there in Babylon along with them. For seventy years the great men of the land were in captivity in Babylon, hundreds of miles from Jerusalem. And for all of that time, Jerusalem fell into decay and disrepair. To make it easier to grasp, let me describe it this way. Jerusalem looked exactly like your home town would look if it went for seventy years with no police force, no sheriff's department, no leaders, no rules, no businesses, and no schools. Do you have that picture in your mind? All the windows would have been smashed out within the first few years, every property vandalized, graffiti everywhere, gangs running wild, drugs sold openly on every street corner, garbage overflowing in the street. And the walls, if it had walls, would all have been broken down, burned, and left lying there in heaps of rubble. It would be a cesspool, a dangerous, filthy, unsafe place.

That is what Jerusalem was like!

Two returns had already taken place. In 538 B.C., Zerrubabel led a group back, and the temple was rebuilt. So the city had one structure that was up and running, and praise God, they at least started with the right one!

In 458 B.C., Ezra the scribe led a return because the people had already begun to neglect the temple worship and backslide into sin. He came back and led a revival and a restoration of temple worship, but the entire city was still in ruins.

So in 444 B.C., God began to move in the heart of a Jewish man hundreds of miles away in Shushan, the palace of Persia. What happened as a result is recorded for us in the book of Nehemiah. This book is a book of adventure and excitement, political intrigue and great danger. It is also a book showing what can be accomplished when one person lays it all on the line to do what needs to be done. May we all be that kind of a "one person!"

Chapter One

When Everything Isn't Enough

Nehemiah 1:1 *The words of Nehemiah the son of Hachaliah. And it came to pass in the month Chisleu, in the twentieth year, as I was in Shushan the palace,* **2** *That Hanani, one of my brethren, came, he and certain men of Judah; and I asked them concerning the Jews that had escaped, which were left of the captivity, and concerning Jerusalem.* **3** *And they said unto me, The remnant that are left of the captivity there in the province are in great affliction and reproach: the wall of Jerusalem also is broken down, and the gates thereof are burned with fire.* **4** *And it came to pass, when I heard these words, that I sat down and wept, and mourned certain days, and fasted, and prayed before the God of heaven,* **5** *And said, I beseech thee, O LORD God of heaven, the great and terrible God, that keepeth covenant and mercy for them that love him and observe his commandments:* **6** *Let thine ear now be attentive, and thine eyes open, that thou mayest hear the prayer of thy servant, which I pray before thee now, day and night, for the children of Israel thy servants, and confess the sins of the children of Israel, which we have sinned against thee: both I and my father's house have sinned.* **7** *We have dealt very corruptly against thee, and have not kept the commandments, nor the statutes, nor the judgments, which thou commandedst thy servant Moses.* **8** *Remember, I* *beseech thee, the word that thou commandedst thy servant Moses, saying, If ye transgress, I will scatter you abroad among the nations:* **9** *But if ye turn unto me, and keep my commandments, and do them; though there were of you cast out unto the uttermost part of the heaven, yet will I gather them from thence, and will bring them unto the place that I have chosen to set my name there.* **10** *Now these are thy servants and thy people, whom thou hast redeemed by thy great power, and by thy strong hand.* **11** *O Lord, I beseech thee, let now thine ear be attentive to the prayer of thy servant, and to the prayer of thy servants, who desire to fear thy name: and prosper, I pray thee, thy servant this day, and grant him mercy in the sight of this man. For I was the king's cupbearer.*

A Sad Condition

Nehemiah 1:1 *The words of Nehemiah the son of Hachaliah. And it came to pass in the month Chisleu, in the twentieth year, as I was in Shushan the palace,* **2** *That Hanani, one of my brethren, came, he and certain men of Judah; and I asked them concerning the Jews that had escaped, which were left of the captivity, and concerning Jerusalem.*

There is another Nehemiah mentioned in Scripture, in Ezra 2:2, but the only place we read about this Nehemiah is in this book that bears his name. But for those of you who love to know the proofs we have that the Bible is indeed the Word of God, he is mentioned in another place. The Elephantine Papyri, discovered in 1903, confirms the historicity of the book of Nehemiah, mentioning both Sanballat (one of the enemies of the book) and Nehemiah by name. It also tells us that Nehemiah ceased to be governor before 408 B.C., making a later date for the writing of the book impossible, confirming that it was written during the time period the Bible lays out for it.[1]

As Nehemiah was in Shushan the palace in their month of Chislue, which is November/December for us, he got a visit from a man named Hanani and some other friends. They had just come from Jerusalem, and Nehemiah wanted to know how things were going there. He was going to get an answer that he would not like:

Nehemiah 1:3 *And they said unto me, The remnant that are left of the captivity there in the province are in great affliction and reproach: the wall of Jerusalem also is broken down, and the gates thereof are burned with fire.*

This report was like a knife to Nehemiah's heart. We are not told if the walls were still broken down from the time of Nebuchadnezzar all those years earlier or if they had been rebuilt sometime along the way and then torn down again. What we do know is that this is not what Nehemiah expected to hear or wanted to hear. The walls were torn down; the gates were burned with fire. As for the people, Hanani described them as being *in great affliction and reproach.* They were being hurt, and they were being mocked.

On March 2, 2010, there was a news story on WBT news, a story by reporter Molly Grantham. It was about a 76-year-old lady who got out of prison ten years earlier. She was an abused wife, going to the hospital dozens of times with broken ribs, busted eye sockets, bloody lips, and battered cheek bones. Twice she tried to run, and he tracked her down and dragged her back both times. He even put a gun to her sister's head and threatened to kill her if she did not stay home. She called the police and pressed charges multiple times, and they never did a thing.

Finally, her son killed the man. But he and a friend and this lady went to prison for it. After 20 years, she was paroled, but she is trying to get a pardon so she can be free to move around. Here is the kicker: the man's brother has gone to the pardon board and made sure that she does not get a pardon. When they interviewed him, he laughed about his brother beating that poor woman and said she deserved it. He said she brought it all on herself and that she "needed the whoopins." This woman was abused and then mocked, and that is exactly the condition the Jews in Jerusalem were in. And this is the condition the devil loves to get God's people and God's work into as well.

A Sorrowful Cry

Nehemiah 1:4 *And it came to pass, when I heard these words, that I sat down and wept, and mourned certain days, and fasted, and prayed before the God of heaven,*

I want you to notice those two words *certain days*. Nehemiah wept, mourned, fasted, and prayed for *certain days*. Let me tell you how long this went on. The king noticed his sorrow in the first verse of chapter two, in the month Nisan, **four months after he started weeping, praying, fasting, mourning.** I do not know how many days a week he fasted or how many hours a day he prayed, but this situation in Jerusalem got to him bad enough that he kept the process going for four months, until God made the king notice! And look how and what he prayed:

Nehemiah 1:5 *And said, I beseech thee, O LORD God of heaven, the great and terrible God, that keepeth covenant and mercy for them that love him and observe his commandments:*

Nehemiah began at a place where it is always good to begin our prayers, with a recognition of the character of God. That is such a vast thing that we can almost start at a different aspect of His character each time we pray.

Sometimes we may begin with an acknowledgment of His mercy.

Sometimes we may begin with an acknowledgment of His ability to provide.

Sometimes we may begin with an acknowledgment of His grace.

In Nehemiah's case, he began with a recognition of the fact that God is *great and terrible*. When we think of terrible, we are thinking usually in negative terms. But the Biblical word for terrible comes from the word "terror," and it means that God is so great and so powerful that anyone in their right mind would fear before Him. You may think that that is a dark and dreary view of God. But not when you are on His side! When you are on His side and your enemies are bigger than you, it is good to know that He is bigger than your enemies!

But Nehemiah went on in verse five to view the softer side of God, the fact that God will keep His promises and show mercy toward those that obey Him. God is not "looking for a reason to destroy us." He is looking for a reason to bless us!

Nehemiah 1:6 *Let thine ear now be attentive, and thine eyes open, that thou mayest hear the prayer of thy servant, which I pray before thee now, day and night, for the children of Israel thy servants, and confess the sins of the children of Israel, which we have sinned against thee: both I and my father's house have sinned.*

Nehemiah was crying out to God for God to both hear his prayer and see him while he was praying. Nehemiah knew that a tear-stained cheek means something to God. Nehemiah reminded God that he was praying day and night. This was not a little five minute prayer at the breakfast table then off to face the day; Nehemiah spent hours every day confessing his sins and the sins of his people and begging God for mercy.

Nehemiah 1:7 *We have dealt very corruptly against thee, and have not kept the commandments, nor the statutes, nor the judgments, which thou commandedst thy servant Moses.*

Nehemiah had something that we desperately need: a clear understanding of how vile our sin really is. Nehemiah said *we have dealt **very corruptly** against thee.* That word corrupt is often used of dead, decaying, putrefying bodies.

When my wife Dana and I first went to Trinidad and Tobago to visit her missionary parents, we were walking down a beach and came across a dog that had been dead for several days. It was swollen up like the Goodyear blimp and had flies crawling all in and out of it. For some reason of which I am still not certain, I chose to throw a rock at it. May I make a suggestion? Never, ever throw a rock at a swollen, putrefying body...

Our sin is like that in God's sight: bloated and corrupt and filthy and just waiting for a chance to explode. And it is supposed to be like that in our sight as well! Unfortunately, the only time our sin ever seems to be corrupt to us is when we get in trouble for it.

Young person, fornication is corrupt even if you do not get pregnant or get a disease.

Sir, pornography is corrupt even if your wife does not find out about it.

Ma'am, your adultery is corrupt even if your husband does not discover it.

Drug user, your using is corrupt even if you manage to hide it from everyone.

Nehemiah had the sense to say, "Our sins are corrupt!"

Nehemiah 1:8 *Remember, I beseech thee, the word that thou commandedst thy servant Moses, saying, If ye transgress, I will scatter you abroad among the nations: 9 But if ye turn unto me, and keep my commandments, and do them; though there were of you cast out unto the uttermost part of the heaven, yet will I gather them from thence, and will bring them unto the place that I have chosen to set my name there.*

At the end of verse seven, Nehemiah had spoken of the Law of Moses that they had disobeyed. Now, in verses eight and nine he asks God to remember a specific promise He made through Moses. He made this promise both in Leviticus 26 and Deuteronomy 4. It was the promise that if they disobeyed, God would scatter them out among the nations, but if after they were scattered they returned to God, He would bring them back to their land.

Nehemiah already knew of two returns from exile, and he wanted there to be a third one, a big one, an effective one, and he wanted to lead it. Remember that, it will become very important in just a few verses.

Nehemiah 1:11 *O Lord, I beseech thee, let now thine ear be attentive to the prayer of thy servant, and to the prayer of thy servants, who desire to fear thy name: and prosper, I pray thee, thy servant this day, and grant him mercy in the sight of this man...*

Nehemiah is now praying about what is in his heart to do. He is praying that God will give him mercy in the sight of the great King Artaxerxes I, because he wants to ask the king to be allowed to go back to Jerusalem and rebuild it. Fortunately, he was praying to the God of whom the Scripture says this:

Proverbs 21:1 *The king's heart is in the hand of the LORD, as the rivers of water: he turneth it whithersoever he will.*

For the heart of a Persian king to be turned in such a way as to allow Nehemiah to go and rebuild the walls, it would definitely be of the Lord.

14

A Stunning Comment

Nehemiah 1:11 *O Lord, I beseech thee, let now thine ear be attentive to the prayer of thy servant, and to the prayer of thy servants, who desire to fear thy name: and prosper, I pray thee, thy servant this day, and grant him mercy in the sight of this man. For I was the king's cupbearer.*

When we think of a cupbearer, we most likely in our modern western minds think of a waiter or waitress, someone who brings us tea at the Golden Corral. Nothing could be farther from the situation of an ancient cupbearer, especially Nehemiah. The cupbearer was the man who was the very closest to the king. The nearest thing we would have to it today would be the office of the Vice President. The cupbearer was also in those days the most trusted man in government. He would usually taste the wine before he gave it to the king, so that the king could never be poisoned. When we get to chapter five, you will find that Nehemiah was a very wealthy man; his position made him rich! The cupbearer was very often second in command in the entire kingdom. It was a position of power, prestige, comfort, luxury, and fame. The only position in the kingdom better than this one was the kingship!

Nehemiah had somehow ended up in the cushiest job and best position possible. He had everything he could ever want:

His meals were the very best...

His housing was the very best...

He was popular, powerful, influential...

He was rich...

Nehemiah had *everything.* But there came a time when *Everything Wasn't Enough!* When Nehemiah realized that God's people were being afflicted and reproached, everything changed for him.

His food did not taste so good anymore...

His bed was not so comfortable anymore...

The accolades and autograph seekers did not matter to him anymore...

His big bank account did not give him joy and comfort anymore...

Nehemiah asked God to allow him to let go of all of that so he could go back to a city that had been desolate for many generations. He asked to be allowed to suffer and sweat and toil and maybe even lose his life to do a work for God. Everything you see him do in this book really is a labor of love! He finally realized that *everything* is actually *nothing* unless you are doing *something* for God.

I wonder, Christian reader, how are you measuring success in your life? Money? Big house? Boat? Fame? Luxury? Big education? Lots of toys?

What about the kids dying and going to Hell within a few miles of your church? Success is doing something to reach them.

What about fellow Christians hurting? Success is doing something to help them.

What about foreign lands that do not have the gospel? Success is getting the gospel to where they are.

What about this country that once was Godly and is now nearly godless? Success is getting a Holy Ghost revival to sweep across our land.

What about our children that are so drawn to this world? Success is seeing them get saved, sanctified, and serious about serving God.

It is about time we got to where Nehemiah did, the place where *"Everything" Isn't Enough...*

Chapter Two
None of Your Business

Nehemiah 2:1 *And it came to pass in the month Nisan, in the twentieth year of Artaxerxes the king, that wine was before him: and I took up the wine, and gave it unto the king. Now I had not been beforetime sad in his presence.* **2** *Wherefore the king said unto me, Why is thy countenance sad, seeing thou art not sick? this is nothing else but sorrow of heart. Then I was very sore afraid,* **3** *And said unto the king, Let the king live for ever: why should not my countenance be sad, when the city, the place of my fathers' sepulchres, lieth waste, and the gates thereof are consumed with fire?* **4** *Then the king said unto me, For what dost thou make request? So I prayed to the God of heaven.* **5** *And I said unto the king, If it please the king, and if thy servant have found favour in thy sight, that thou wouldest send me unto Judah, unto the city of my fathers' sepulchres, that I may build it.* **6** *And the king said unto me, (the queen also sitting by him,) For how long shall thy journey be? and when wilt thou return? So it pleased the king to send me; and I set him a time.* **7** *Moreover I said unto the king, If it please the king, let letters be given me to the governors beyond the river, that they may convey me over till I come into Judah;* **8** *And a letter unto Asaph the keeper of the king's forest, that he may give me timber to make beams for the gates of the palace which appertained to the house, and for the wall of the city, and for the house that I shall enter into. And the king granted me, according to the good hand* *of my God upon me. 9 Then I came to the governors beyond the river, and gave them the king's letters. Now the king had sent captains of the army and horsemen with me. 10 When Sanballat the Horonite, and Tobiah the servant, the Ammonite, heard of it, it grieved them exceedingly that there was come a man to seek the welfare of the children of Israel. 11 So I came to Jerusalem, and was there three days. 12 And I arose in the night, I and some few men with me; neither told I any man what my God had put in my heart to do at Jerusalem: neither was there any beast with me, save the beast that I rode upon. 13 And I went out by night by the gate of the valley, even before the dragon well, and to the dung port, and viewed the walls of Jerusalem, which were broken down, and the gates thereof were consumed with fire. 14 Then I went on to the gate of the fountain, and to the king's pool: but there was no place for the beast that was under me to pass. 15 Then went I up in the night by the brook, and viewed the wall, and turned back, and entered by the gate of the valley, and so returned. 16 And the rulers knew not whither I went, or what I did; neither had I as yet told it to the Jews, nor to the priests, nor to the nobles, nor to the rulers, nor to the rest that did the work. 17 Then said I unto them, Ye see the distress that we are in, how Jerusalem lieth waste, and the gates thereof are burned with fire: come, and let us build up the wall of Jerusalem, that we be no more a reproach. 18 Then I told them of the hand of my God which was good upon me; as also the king's words that he had spoken unto me. And they said, Let us rise up and build. So they strengthened their hands for this good work. 19 But when Sanballat the Horonite, and Tobiah the servant, the Ammonite, and Geshem the Arabian, heard it, they laughed us to scorn, and despised us, and said, What is this thing that ye do? will ye rebel against the king? 20 Then answered I them, and said unto them, The God of heaven, he will prosper us; therefore we his servants will arise and build: but ye have no portion, nor right, nor memorial, in Jerusalem.*

As we saw in chapter one, in 444 B.C., God began to move in the heart of a Jewish man hundreds of miles away from Jerusalem in Shushan, the palace of Persia. This man named Nehemiah, a man in a very comfortable position as the king's cupbearer, received word that the walls and city of Jerusalem were laying in ruins and that the people were being savaged.

That broke his heart. So he fasted, prayed, and begged God to allow him and empower him to fix things. What happened as a result is recorded for us in the book of Nehemiah. This book is a book of adventure and excitement, political intrigue and great danger. It is also a book showing what can be accomplished when one person lays it all on the line to do what needs to be done. Nehemiah got a good start on that in chapter one, and the results would begin to show in chapter two.

A Scary Position

Nehemiah 2:1 *And it came to pass in the month Nisan, in the twentieth year of Artaxerxes the king, that wine was before him: and I took up the wine, and gave it unto the king. Now I had not been beforetime sad in his presence.*

This verse tells us a great deal about the character of Nehemiah. In order for Nehemiah to have arrived at this exalted position, he had been in the presence of the king for a very long time. This was not the job of a newcomer off the street. Yet for all the time the king had observed him, Nehemiah had never been sad in his presence.

Question: do you think that he never had any reason to be sad? Of course not. Nehemiah had reasons to be sad, but chose to be happy! In other words, he is the exact opposite of some very dear folks that I know and love, and doubtless some very dear folks that you know and love, who choose to be sad when there are reasons to be happy!

May I give some excellent advice? One: choose to be happy. Two: make sadness a rare, temporary thing, shed your tears, and then choose to be happy again. Three: never marry anyone who chooses to be sad, or you will spend the rest of your life sad along with them. Four: during the times you are happy, use Facebook. During the times you are sad, use a paperback book, a library book, a comic book, any other book other than Facebook! Five: if you choose to be sad instead of happy, please do not infect any of my church people with your misery. They have enough to deal with without you adding to their problems.

Six: if you are angry at my list of helpful suggestions, get over it and choose to be happy!

Nehemiah 2:2 *Wherefore the king said unto me, Why is thy countenance sad, seeing thou art not sick? this is nothing else but sorrow of heart. Then I was very sore afraid,*

Why would Nehemiah be afraid? Because the Persian kings were not in the habit of allowing mourning in their presence. We learned this from the book of Esther:

Esther 4:1 *When Mordecai perceived all that was done, Mordecai rent his clothes, and put on sackcloth with ashes, and went out into the midst of the city, and cried with a loud and a bitter cry;* **2** *And came even before the king's gate: for none might enter into the king's gate clothed with sackcloth.*

Nehemiah knew that his life was at risk! He needed God to soften the heart of the most powerful man on earth:

Nehemiah 2:3 *And said unto the king, Let the king live for ever: why should not my countenance be sad, when the city, the place of my fathers' sepulchres, lieth waste, and the gates thereof are consumed with fire?*

This was a jaw-dropping moment. Why should the Persian king care about the burned city of his captives? Nehemiah could very well have been writing his own death warrant by that admission. But again, for him, everything wasn't enough. If he could not do a work for God, nothing else mattered. This truly was a scary position...

A Secret Prayer

Nehemiah 2:4 *Then the king said unto me, For what dost thou make request? So I prayed to the God of heaven.*

This was on the spur of the moment, unexpected, unplanned. In the twinkling of an eye Nehemiah was able, standing right where he was, to fire off a secret prayer to Heaven and have it heard. I wonder, is your life in such a condition that you could do that? Terrifying times do not usually come announced; they normally come unannounced. If you are not prepared to pray and be heard during moments when the world is well, then you will certainly not be prepared to pray when you are surprised at the world falling apart!

A Supernatural Provision

Nehemiah 2:5 *And I said unto the king, If it please the king, and if thy servant have found favour in thy sight, that thou wouldest send me unto Judah, unto the city of my fathers' sepulchres, that I may build it.*

There was absolutely no reason for Artaxerxes to grant this request; there was no benefit to himself or his kingdom in it. In fact, he would be losing part of his own "life insurance" by granting it, since Nehemiah was the one responsible for making sure he never got poisoned!

Nehemiah 2:6 *And the king said unto me, (the queen also sitting by him,) For how long shall thy journey be? and when wilt thou return? So it pleased the king to send me; and I set him a time.*

There is an unusual thing to notice in this verse. In parenthesis, notice those words *the queen also sitting by him.* Why is that there? Persian queens did not normally sit by their husbands. If you remember the story of Esther, they had to be called before his presence or risk death coming uninvited. So to have her there was a very unusual thing, a thing just not done. Why was it done here? I agree with Jamison, Faussett, and Brown, this might have been a queen whose name you know very well, it was probably Esther herself! After the episode with wicked Haman, Artaxerxes probably wanted her nearby. If so, that is just one more evidence of the awesome planning of God, to have the sweet Jewish queen there beside the Persian king when his Jewish subject asked for such a great thing!

One way or the other, the improbable request was granted.

Nehemiah 2:7 *Moreover I said unto the king, If it please the king, let letters be given me to the governors beyond the river, that they may convey me over till I come into Judah;* **8** *And a letter unto Asaph the keeper of the king's forest, that he may give me timber to make beams for the gates of the palace which appertained to the house, and for the wall of the city, and for the house that I shall enter into. And the king granted me, according to the good hand of my God upon me.*

Once Artaxerxes granted his main request, Nehemiah asked for everything else he would need. The request list was huge, but the king granted it all! Why? Because of (v.8) *the good hand of my God.* Whenever mankind starts being truly generous with you, God is behind it.

A Spiteful Pair

Nehemiah 2:9 *Then I came to the governors beyond the river, and gave them the king's letters. Now the king had sent captains of the army and horsemen with me.* **10** *When Sanballat the Horonite, and Tobiah the servant, the Ammonite, heard of it, it grieved them exceedingly that there was come a man to seek the welfare of the children of Israel.*

When Nehemiah came into Jerusalem he came in with a bang, accompanied by the army and the horsemen. He was prepared for his venture, which is a great thing for us to mimic. Whatever we are going to do for the Lord deserves our preparation and our might!

Nehemiah was running well. But then came the first two enemies, a spiteful pair. One was Sanballat the Horonite, the ring-leader throughout the book. Being from Horonaim, he was a Moabite. Along with him was Tobiah, a servant, an Ammonite. Imagine that! Moab and Ammon together again giving Israel fits. The sins of Lot still visited upon Israel all those years later, as is usually the case with sin. Sin often outlasts the entire generation that started it.

These two were really, really upset over a terrible thing: someone had come along who actually cared about what happened to God's people and wanted to make things better for them!

This is something you actually see in churches from time to time. A little church will putter along for years with a handful of people, never doing anything for God or the people God loves, like children. Then somehow a man of God gets in there with a burden to win souls and train kids and put some life back in the church, and you would think Satan has walked into their midst! How dare anyone upset the apple cart of a church that is pleased by its own slow descent into death!

A Survey of the Problem

Nehemiah 2:11 *So I came to Jerusalem, and was there three days.* **12** *And I arose in the night, I and some few men with me; neither told I any man what my God had put in my heart to do at Jerusalem: neither was there any beast with me, save the beast that I rode upon.*

Why is it that Nehemiah did not yet tell anyone what he wanted to do? One of the quickest ways to have something destroyed before it even gets started is summed up in a saying from World War II: *Loose lips sink ships.* People need to learn to treat information like money. Only hand it out <u>when you are supposed to</u> and <u>to whom you are supposed to</u>. Pastors usually know some very nice people that they can never, ever put in any positions of leadership, because they cannot keep confidential information. Nehemiah kept his lips sealed. He took a few good men with him and only one animal to ride on, so as not to attract attention.

Nehemiah 2:13 *And I went out by night by the gate of the valley, even before the dragon well, and to the dung port, and viewed the walls of Jerusalem, which were broken down, and the gates thereof were consumed with fire.* **14** *Then I went on to the gate of the fountain, and to the king's pool: but there was no place for the beast that was under me to pass.*

Nehemiah went across the valley to a place called the Dragon Well where he could get a good view of the city walls. He came back and started a lap around them for a close up view. He got all the way to Solomon's Pool, which had once been a glorious place, and found that there was so much rubble piled up that he could not get his beast through. But rather than give up, he kept going by another path:

Nehemiah 2:15 *Then went I up in the night by the brook, and viewed the wall, and turned back, and entered by the gate of the valley, and so returned.*

From Solomon's Pool he went over by the Brook Kidron to view the wall from there. Then he went back into the city by way of the Gate of the Valley. Verse thirteen says that he started his trip through that very same Gate of the Valley. He made his way all the way around the entire city. He did a very thorough job of checking things out. That is another good example to follow. Thoroughness ought to be something we practice in everything we do!

Nehemiah 2:16 *And the rulers knew not whither I went, or what I did; neither had I as yet told it to the Jews, nor to the priests, nor to the nobles, nor to the rulers, nor to the rest that did the work.*

The survey was done, but no one yet knew what he was up to. One man had a burden, one man now had good knowledge of what lay ahead, one man had a vision, but one man cannot do much unless he can motivate others to join in.

A Starting Point

Nehemiah 2:17 _Then_ (I emphasize that word for a reason, I am not going to say why yet, I just want you to remember it for now) *said I unto them, Ye see the distress that we are in, how Jerusalem lieth waste, and the gates thereof are burned with fire: come, and let us build up the wall of Jerusalem, that we be no more a reproach.*

Nehemiah used as a starting point a presentation of the desperate need. But now notice this:

Nehemiah 2:18a _Then_ *I told them of the hand of my God which was good upon me; as also the king's words that he had spoken unto me...*

Why the second "then?" God does everything for a reason. The normal way you would see this written would be something like this:

"Then said I unto them, Ye see the distress that we are in, how Jerusalem lieth waste, and the gates thereof are burned with fire: come, and let us build up the wall of Jerusalem, that we be no more a reproach. The hand of my God has been good upon me; as also the king's words that he had spoken unto me. And they said, Let us rise up and build. So they strengthened their hands for this good work."

That would be normal. The second "then" at the beginning of verse eighteen tells me that just hearing the need and seeing the desperate condition had not sealed the deal with them. They had been there longer than he had, they already knew how bad things were. If that had not motivated them to do something by now, just hearing it again from someone else

24

probably was not going to change things. I am sure Nehemiah saw that written on their faces. So "then" he told them of *the hand of my God which was good upon me; as also the king's words that he had spoken unto me...*

What people cannot be motivated to do by seeing the greatness of the problem, they can often be motivated to do by seeing the greatness of God. I am all in favor of pointing out the problems in society and church and homes, but I am even more in favor of pointing out that our God is great enough to fix things if we will just let Him use us.

Nehemiah 2:18 *Then I told them of the hand of my God which was good upon me; as also the king's words that he had spoken unto me. And they said, Let us rise up and build. So they strengthened their hands for this good work.*

When they saw the greatness of God, they started rolling up their sleeves.

A Straight Putdown

Nehemiah 2:19 *But when Sanballat the Horonite, and Tobiah the servant, the Ammonite, and Geshem the Arabian, heard it, they laughed us to scorn, and despised us, and said, What is this thing that ye do? will ye rebel against the king?*

To our two original enemies we now add Geshem the Arabian, who at other times in the book will be called "Gashmu." They were just like us, we take James and make Jim out of it; we take Robert and make Bob out of it. So now there are three enemy leaders to contend with. These three hear the plans of Nehemiah, and they do three things that enemies usually do:

One, they made fun of them. They *laughed us to scorn.*

Two, they looked down their noses at them. They *despised us.*

Three, they assumed a lie without asking for the truth. *What is this thing that ye do? will ye rebel against the king?*

No, they had permission from the king. Never mind that, though, people would usually rather assume a lie than ask for the truth. So Nehemiah now has a choice to make. The enemies have arrived, and he must decide what to do with them.

Perhaps he could take the diplomatic approach: "Hi, guys, I realize you can't stand us. Come on over for tea and I'll let you explain to me what it is you hate about us so I can understand you better."

That is not the approach Nehemiah took. You see, these enemies had already very clearly let it be known that they were not interested in anything but hindering what needed to be done. So Nehemiah took an approach based on that knowledge. The approach he took was the *None of Your Business!* approach. They had asked a question; *What is this thing that ye do?* Here was his answer:

Nehemiah 2:20 *Then answered I them, and said unto them, The God of heaven, he will prosper us; therefore we his servants will arise and build: but ye have no portion, nor right, nor memorial, in Jerusalem.*

What would be a good summary of that? "We are about to have a building project and you do not have any need to know what or where or how or how long. God is on our side, and the details and outcome are *None of Your Business!*"

Since I am a pastor, may I put this in church terms? I am always amazed at people who leave church, go somewhere else, and yet still want to have influence in what goes on in the church they left. *It's none of their business!*

I am amazed when people leave church, go somewhere else, yet instead of making friends with people over there and leaving my folks alone, always want to call and come over and Facebook and do lunch, all for the purpose of prying, questioning, and trying to find out what is going on now that they are gone. *It's none of their business!*

If trouble-making people are going to go away, I want them to actually *go away!* It would probably be helpful if all church-going Christians learned how to say those words. Practice them with me:

Go away! Go away! Go away! Go away! Go away!

Try this one, the one Nehemiah used:

It's none of your business! It's none of your business! It's none of your business! It's none of your business!

Isn't that nice?

Nehemiah was successful for God largely because he knew who was going to be a help and he knew who was going to be a hindrance and he treated them as such. Among those who are going to help not all are as strong, not all are as advanced, not all are as capable. That is fine; there is no problem at all with that. But hear me: when it comes to the work of God, there are always going to be those who are actually *trying* to cause problems. And they will always try to do so from within, if they can, because that is the best place from which to cause problems. Those kind of people you better be able to identify, and you better be ready to stick a hand in their face and give them the big *None of Your Business!*

Chapter Three
The Tale of the Tape

Nehemiah 3:1 *Then Eliashib the high priest rose up with his brethren the priests, and they builded the sheep gate; they sanctified it, and set up the doors of it; even unto the tower of Meah they sanctified it, unto the tower of Hananeel.* **2** *And next unto him builded the men of Jericho. And next to them builded Zaccur the son of Imri.* **3** *But the fish gate did the sons of Hassenaah build, who also laid the beams thereof, and set up the doors thereof, the locks thereof, and the bars thereof.* **4** *And next unto them repaired Meremoth the son of Urijah, the son of Koz. And next unto them repaired Meshullam the son of Berechiah, the son of Meshezabeel. And next unto them repaired Zadok the son of Baana.* **5** *And next unto them the Tekoites repaired; but their nobles put not their necks to the work of their Lord.* **6** *Moreover the old gate repaired Jehoiada the son of Paseah, and Meshullam the son of Besodeiah; they laid the beams thereof, and set up the doors thereof, and the locks thereof, and the bars thereof.* **7** *And next unto them repaired Melatiah the Gibeonite, and Jadon the Meronothite, the men of Gibeon, and of Mizpah, unto the throne of the governor on this side the river.* **8** *Next unto him repaired Uzziel the son of Harhaiah, of the goldsmiths. Next unto him also repaired Hananiah the son of one of the apothecaries, and they fortified Jerusalem unto the broad wall.* **9** *And next unto them repaired Rephaiah the son of Hur, the ruler of the half part of Jerusalem.*

10 *And next unto them repaired Jedaiah the son of Harumaph, even over against his house. And next unto him repaired Hattush the son of Hashabniah.* **11** *Malchijah the son of Harim, and Hashub the son of Pahathmoab, repaired the other piece, and the tower of the furnaces.* **12** *And next unto him repaired Shallum the son of Halohesh, the ruler of the half part of Jerusalem, he and his daughters.* **13** *The valley gate repaired Hanun, and the inhabitants of Zanoah; they built it, and set up the doors thereof, the locks thereof, and the bars thereof, and a thousand cubits on the wall unto the dung gate.* **14** *But the dung gate repaired Malchiah the son of Rechab, the ruler of part of Bethhaccerem; he built it, and set up the doors thereof, the locks thereof, and the bars thereof.* **15** *But the gate of the fountain repaired Shallun the son of Colhozeh, the ruler of part of Mizpah; he built it, and covered it, and set up the doors thereof, the locks thereof, and the bars thereof, and the wall of the pool of Siloah by the king's garden, and unto the stairs that go down from the city of David.* **16** *After him repaired Nehemiah the son of Azbuk, the ruler of the half part of Bethzur, unto the place over against the sepulchres of David, and to the pool that was made, and unto the house of the mighty.* **17** *After him repaired the Levites, Rehum the son of Bani. Next unto him repaired Hashabiah, the ruler of the half part of Keilah, in his part.* **18** *After him repaired their brethren, Bavai the son of Henadad, the ruler of the half part of Keilah.* **19** *And next to him repaired Ezer the son of Jeshua, the ruler of Mizpah, another piece over against the going up to the armoury at the turning of the wall.* **20** *After him Baruch the son of Zabbai earnestly repaired the other piece, from the turning of the wall unto the door of the house of Eliashib the high priest.* **21** *After him repaired Meremoth the son of Urijah the son of Koz another piece, from the door of the house of Eliashib even to the end of the house of Eliashib.* **22** *And after him repaired the priests, the men of the plain.* **23** *After him repaired Benjamin and Hashub over against their house. After him repaired Azariah the son of Maaseiah the son of Ananiah by his house.* **24** *After him repaired Binnui the son of Henadad another piece, from the house of Azariah unto the turning of the wall, even unto the corner.* **25** *Palal the son of Uzai, over against the turning of the wall, and the tower which* *lieth out from the king's high house, that was by the court of the prison. After him Pedaiah the son of Parosh.* **26** *Moreover the Nethinims dwelt in Ophel, unto the place over against the water gate toward the east, and the tower that lieth out.* **27** *After them the Tekoites repaired another piece, over against the great tower that lieth out, even unto the wall of Ophel.* **28** *From above the horse gate repaired the priests, every one over against his house.* **29** *After them repaired Zadok the son of Immer over against his house. After him repaired also Shemaiah the son of Shechaniah, the keeper of the east gate.* **30** *After him repaired Hananiah the son of Shelemiah, and Hanun the sixth son of Zalaph, another piece. After him repaired Meshullam the son of Berechiah over against his chamber.* **31** *After him repaired Malchiah the goldsmith's son unto the place of the Nethinims, and of the merchants, over against the gate Miphkad, and to the going up of the corner.* **32** *And between the going up of the corner unto the sheep gate repaired the goldsmiths and the merchants.*

In chapter one, God moved on the heart of a man with a comfortable life and a comfortable job, a Jew by the name of Nehemiah. Nehemiah became burdened to rebuild the ravaged walls of Jerusalem. So in chapter two, after four months of praying, God had the king notice Nehemiah's sad countenance and ask him what was wrong. Nehemiah ended up being granted permission to go back and rebuild the walls and was also granted the material from the king's forests to do so.

But it was also in chapter two that enemies reared their heads. Chapter two verse ten says:

Nehemiah 2:10 *When Sanballat the Horonite, and Tobiah the servant, the Ammonite, heard of it, it grieved them exceedingly that there was come a man to seek the welfare of the children of Israel.*

It has always grieved the devil and his crowd whenever anyone seeks the welfare of the children of Israel.

When Nehemiah arrived he did a secret, night-time inspection of the city to see what needed to be done. Then he told the rulers of the city what he had in mind and they readily agreed to do the job. At that point a third enemy joined in with Sanballat and Tobiah, a man named Geshem. Undaunted, Nehemiah told them to back off, and that he was going to see the walls rebuilt, and that everything going on was really none of their business.

In chapter three we will see a detailed account of who built what.

Nehemiah 3:1 *Then Eliashib the high priest rose up with his brethren the priests, and they builded the sheep gate; they sanctified it, and set up the doors of it; even unto the tower of Meah they sanctified it, unto the tower of Hananeel.*

The first thing we should notice is preachers who were willing to work. The high priest and the priests working under him got into the mix and physically labored to build the wall. Every preacher should be willing to work with his mind and his mouth, but he should also be willing to work with his arms and his back unless he is too aged or infirmed to do so!

Notice also that the entire project started with the Sheep Gate, which was the gate where the sacrifices were brought in. This was by design. It was intended to show the importance of giving in our worship.

Nehemiah 3:2 *And next unto him builded the men of Jericho. And next to them builded Zaccur the son of Imri.*

Now we see a group of out-of-towners building in Jerusalem. These were people who were thinking not just of themselves, but of others.

Nehemiah 3:3 *But the fish gate did the sons of Hassenaah build, who also laid the beams thereof, and set up the doors thereof, the locks thereof, and the bars thereof. 4 And next unto them repaired Meremoth the son of Urijah, the son of Koz. And next unto them repaired Meshullam the son of Berechiah, the son of Meshezabeel. And next unto them repaired Zadok the son of Baana. 5 And next unto them the Tekoites repaired; but their nobles put not their necks to the work of their Lord.*

Verse five contains one of the sharpest indictments I can think of. The Tekoites were working, building, sweating, laboring. But the noblemen of Tekoa, the "upper crust" of their crowd, felt like such work was beneath them. That is a sorry, steaming, stinking sack of humanity right there.

Oh, I'm so sorry! I didn't realize your precious hands were too important to hold a shovel or a hammer. We wouldn't want you to get a blister...

Oh, I'm sorry! My nursery captain should have known better than to ask you for help in the nursery. Changing poopy diapers is a job for "regular people" to do, not someone like you...

Nehemiah 3:8 *Next unto him repaired Uzziel the son of Harhaiah, of the goldsmiths. Next unto him also repaired Hananiah the son of one of the apothecaries, and they fortified Jerusalem unto the broad wall.*

Goldsmiths and apothecaries (fragrance makers) repaired this section. These were the artistic, high-paid, extremely skilled kind of workers. Not the kind of people that would normally be swinging pick axes. They were, though, people who were willing to work "outside of their job description" to get the project done. My church was blessed by an electrician who did not mind laying vinyl floor tiles in a bathroom. People like that are easy to love!

Nehemiah 3:9 *And next unto them repaired Rephaiah the son of Hur, the ruler of the half part of Jerusalem.*

As far as we can tell, Jerusalem at this point in time was divided into two parts (one for Judah, one for Benjamin) and each half had a ruler. Rephaiah was one of those two important men, yet he was right in there with everyone else doing his part. There is no "caste system" in the work of God!

Nehemiah 3:10 *And next unto them repaired Jedaiah the son of Harumaph, even over against his house. And next unto him repaired Hattush the son of Hashabniah.*

Jedaiah repaired the wall by his own house. This is not a selfish thing, it had to be done just like everything else! How hypocritical is it when a person wants to "fix everyone else's problems" but will not deal with their own!

Nehemiah 3:11 *Malchijah the son of Harim, and Hashub the son of Pahathmoab, repaired the other piece, and the tower of the furnaces.* **12** *And next unto him repaired Shallum the son of Halohesh, the ruler of the half part of Jerusalem, he and his daughters.*

Here we have the ruler of the other half of Jerusalem working at it. But what I find even more interesting is that his daughters were working right alongside him!

The expensive commentaries on my office shelves say "they built by paying for part of the expenses." That is NOT what the Bible says! It says their daddy worked, and they worked with him. It seems as though this man never had any boys, but he raised girls who were as good as any boys and just as willing to get dirt under their finger nails if that is what it took to get the wall done. There is something amazing about a girl who is feminine, pretty, proper, and at the same time can haul block if it comes right down to it.

Nehemiah 3:13 *The valley gate repaired Hanun, and the inhabitants of Zanoah; they built it, and set up the doors thereof, the locks thereof, and the bars thereof, and a thousand cubits on the wall unto the dung gate.*

These men did 1,500 feet of the wall by themselves! Thank God for those who do what little bit they can, but thank God also for those who have the strength and ability to do mountains of work.

Nehemiah 3:14 *But the dung gate repaired Malchiah the son of Rechab, the ruler of part of Bethhaccerem; he built it, and set up the doors thereof, the locks thereof, and the bars thereof.*

As you might have guessed from the name, there was nothing glorious about the Dung Gate. It was the gate that all of the trash of the city came through to be dumped in the valley. A very important man, a ruler, rebuilt this nasty site. Thank God for people who do not mind doing the dirty jobs!

Nehemiah 3:15 *But the gate of the fountain repaired Shallun the son of Colhozeh, the ruler of part of Mizpah; he built it, and covered it, and set up the doors thereof, the locks thereof, and the bars thereof, and the wall of the pool of Siloah by the king's garden, and unto the stairs that go down from the city of David.* **16** *After him repaired Nehemiah the son of Azbuk, the ruler of the half part of Bethzur, unto the place over against the sepulchres of David, and to the pool that was made, and unto the house of the mighty.*

These are the men that built to and through the place where the stairs of the city were. In other words, they built on the uneven ground. Jerusalem is built on hilly ground, and some people had to build in hilly, uneven places. Doing that requires an extra set of skills. These were people who knew what they were doing and were willing to do it. You could trust them to do a complicated job right. If you have the skills to do complicated tasks, you are needed in the service of the Lord. Use those skills for God every time you get the opportunity!

Nehemiah 3:17 *After him repaired the Levites, Rehum the son of Bani. Next unto him repaired Hashabiah, the ruler of the half part of Keilah, in his part.* **18** *After him repaired their brethren, Bavai the son of Henadad, the ruler of the half part of Keilah.*

Here are more men that repaired, with not much detail or fanfare given. But notice the interesting contrast in the next two verses:

Nehemiah 3:19 *And next to him repaired Ezer the son of Jeshua, the ruler of Mizpah, another piece over against the going up to the armoury at the turning of the wall.* **20** *After him Baruch the son of Zabbai earnestly repaired the other piece, from the turning of the wall unto the door of the house of Eliashib the high priest.*

The first man, Ezer, repaired the piece of the wall leading up to the turn mentioned here. The second man, Baruch, repaired the piece of the wall leading away from the turn. So they repaired very similar pieces of the wall. But what one difference do you notice? They both repaired, but Baruch *earnestly repaired*. This guy was the kind of guy that had a determined look on his face, and ran from one place to the next, and took shorter breaks than everybody else, and got there earlier, and stayed up later. This man had the kind of work ethic that every Christian ought to have no matter what job they are doing, spiritual or secular!

Nehemiah 3:21 *After him repaired Meremoth the son of Urijah the son of Koz another piece, from the door of the house of Eliashib even to the end of the house of Eliashib.* **22** *And after him repaired the priests, the men of the plain.*

Here you have an odd thing, preachers that did not have to be recognized by name!

Nehemiah 3:23 *After him repaired Benjamin and Hashub over against their house. After him repaired Azariah the son of Maaseiah the son of Ananiah by his house.* **24** *After him repaired Binnui the son of Henadad another piece, from the house of Azariah unto the turning of the wall, even unto the corner.* **25** *Palal the son of Uzai, over against the turning of the wall, and the tower which lieth out from the king's high house, that was by the court of the prison. After him Pedaiah the son of Parosh.*

Some of these men labored on a section of the wall attached to the prison. They clearly were not worried about becoming inmates themselves! A clear conscience will allow you to do work that others fear to do.

Nehemiah 3:26 *Moreover the Nethinims dwelt in Ophel, unto the place over against the water gate toward the east, and the tower that lieth out.*

There are no errors in the Bible. Many commentaries insert the words "they repaired unto" in this verse. But that is not what the Bible says. It says of everyone else "they repaired" this or that, but of the Nethinims it simply says "moreover the Nethinims dwelt" in Ophel. Just from the words of this verse, it certainly seems that they lived there but were not engaged in the rebuilding process! In other words, it at least appears that they were freeloaders, enjoying the benefits of all that went on without contributing to all that went on.

Nehemiah 3:27 *After them the Tekoites repaired another piece, over against the great tower that lieth out, even unto the wall of Ophel.*

Now this I really like. Do you remember what we saw about the Tekoites?

Nehemiah 3:5 *And next unto them the Tekoites repaired; but their nobles put not their necks to the work of their Lord.*

The Tekoites were the good guys with the "too good for this kind of thing" rulers. Yet in spite of their weasely leaders, they not only repaired their part, they went on and found another part to do! No matter how bad your mom/dad/boss/ preacher/teacher/president/ whatever is, you do not have to do nothing just because those leading you have done nothing.

Nehemiah 3:28 *From above the horse gate repaired the priests, every one over against his house.* **29** *After them repaired Zadok the son of Immer over against his house. After him repaired also Shemaiah the son of Shechaniah, the keeper of the east gate.* **30** *After him repaired Hananiah the son of Shelemiah, and Hanun the sixth son of Zalaph, another piece. After him repaired Meshullam the son of Berechiah over against his chamber.*

This man had five older brothers, and they are not mentioned among the workers. Big brothers are not doing their part, but Hanun is doing more than his part.

Nehemiah 3:13 *The valley gate repaired **Hanun**, and the inhabitants of Zanoah; they built it, and set up the doors thereof, the locks thereof, and the bars thereof, and a thousand cubits on the wall unto the dung gate.*

His siblings are not doing right, but he is doing extra right. Some of you may have to ignore the bad example of your own brothers and sisters and be completely different from them.

Nehemiah 3:31 *After him repaired Malchiah the goldsmith's son unto the place of the Nethinims, and of the merchants, over against the gate Miphkad, and to the going up of the corner.* **32** *And between the going up of the corner unto the sheep gate repaired the goldsmiths and the merchants.*

These men had the privilege of being the "closers." They got to repair the last piece.

Many men in this chapter did not have anything specific said about them, other than that "they repaired." They are just as important as all the rest. They did not all repair 1,500 feet, but everyone who actually dug in and worked played a vital role in getting the entire thing done.

There is something for everyone to do in serving God. Not everyone can stand behind the pulpit, but everyone can and should do something. So here is a question: if God were writing one more chapter of Scripture, about the work of God going on in your church, what would He write, or not write, about you?

Chapter Four
A Mind to Work

Nehemiah 4:1 *But it came to pass, that when Sanballat heard that we builded the wall, he was wroth, and took great indignation, and mocked the Jews. 2 And he spake before his brethren and the army of Samaria, and said, What do these feeble Jews? will they fortify themselves? will they sacrifice? will they make an end in a day? will they revive the stones out of the heaps of the rubbish which are burned? 3 Now Tobiah the Ammonite was by him, and he said, Even that which they build, if a fox go up, he shall even break down their stone wall. 4 Hear, O our God; for we are despised: and turn their reproach upon their own head, and give them for a prey in the land of captivity: 5 And cover not their iniquity, and let not their sin be blotted out from before thee: for they have provoked thee to anger before the builders. 6 So built we the wall; and all the wall was joined together unto the half thereof: for the people had a mind to work. 7 But it came to pass, that when Sanballat, and Tobiah, and the Arabians, and the Ammonites, and the Ashdodites, heard that the walls of Jerusalem were made up, and that the breaches began to be stopped, then they were very wroth, 8 And conspired all of them together to come and to fight against Jerusalem, and to hinder it. 9 Nevertheless we made our prayer unto our God, and set a watch against them day and night, because of them. 10 And Judah said, The strength of the bearers of burdens is decayed, and there is much rubbish; so that we are not able to* build the wall. **11** *And our adversaries said, They shall not know, neither see, till we come in the midst among them, and slay them, and cause the work to cease.* **12** *And it came to pass, that when the Jews which dwelt by them came, they said unto us ten times, From all places whence ye shall return unto us they will be upon you.* **13** *Therefore set I in the lower places behind the wall, and on the higher places, I even set the people after their families with their swords, their spears, and their bows.* **14** *And I looked, and rose up, and said unto the nobles, and to the rulers, and to the rest of the people, Be not ye afraid of them: remember the Lord, which is great and terrible, and fight for your brethren, your sons, and your daughters, your wives, and your houses.* **15** *And it came to pass, when our enemies heard that it was known unto us, and God had brought their counsel to nought, that we returned all of us to the wall, every one unto his work.* **16** *And it came to pass from that time forth, that the half of my servants wrought in the work, and the other half of them held both the spears, the shields, and the bows, and the habergeons; and the rulers were behind all the house of Judah.* **17** *They which builded on the wall, and they that bare burdens, with those that laded, every one with one of his hands wrought in the work, and with the other hand held a weapon.* **18** *For the builders, every one had his sword girded by his side, and so builded. And he that sounded the trumpet was by me.* **19** *And I said unto the nobles, and to the rulers, and to the rest of the people, The work is great and large, and we are separated upon the wall, one far from another.* **20** *In what place therefore ye hear the sound of the trumpet, resort ye thither unto us: our God shall fight for us.* **21** *So we laboured in the work: and half of them held the spears from the rising of the morning till the stars appeared.* **22** *Likewise at the same time said I unto the people, Let every one with his servant lodge within Jerusalem, that in the night they may be a guard to us, and labour on the day.* **23** *So neither I, nor my brethren, nor my servants, nor the men of the guard which followed me, none of us put off our clothes, saving that every one put them off for washing.*

In chapter one God moved on the heart of a man with a comfortable life and a comfortable job, a Jew by the name of Nehemiah. Nehemiah became burdened to rebuild the ravaged walls of Jerusalem. So in chapter two, after four months of praying, God had the king notice Nehemiah's sad countenance and ask him what was wrong. Nehemiah ended up being granted permission to go back and rebuild the walls, and also was granted the material from the king's forests to do so.

But it was also in chapter two that enemies reared their heads. Chapter two verse ten says:

Nehemiah 2:10 *When Sanballat the Horonite, and Tobiah the servant, the Ammonite, heard of it, it grieved them exceedingly that there was come a man to seek the welfare of the children of Israel.*

It has always grieved the devil and his crowd whenever anyone seeks the welfare of the children of Israel.

When Nehemiah arrived, he did a secret, night-time inspection of the city to see what needed to be done. Then he told the rulers of the city what he had in mind, and they readily agreed to do the job. At that point, a third enemy joined in with Sanballat and Tobiah, a man named Geshem. Undaunted, Nehemiah told them to back off, and that he was going to see the walls rebuilt.

In chapter three, we read a detailed account of the people who engaged in the building and of the gates and portions of the wall that they built. And that brings us to chapter four, where we find some people with a mind to work.

The Worriers

To "worry" something means to shake it up, to distress it. When a dog shakes a rag toy back and forth, he is described as "worrying" it. Nehemiah had to deal with some professional worriers, some people who really knew how to shake other people up.

Nehemiah 4:1 *But it came to pass, that when Sanballat heard that we builded the wall, he was wroth, and took great indignation, and mocked the Jews.*

What you see in verse one was a blessing in every way. People do not often think of being mocked as a blessing, but many times it is, and this was clearly one of those times in at least two ways. First of all, in the verses to follow, you can see that this mockery spurred the Jews on, it riled them up, it got them going.

When Michael Jordan was in his prime, a hot-shot rookie named J. R. Rider dunked over him. But then he made a fatal mistake: he taunted Michael all the way down court, wagging his finger and bobbing his head at him. Michael then scored twenty-three unanswered points, and the coach of that rookie benched him for quite a while and told him that if he ever did that to Michael Jordan again, he would cut him from the team!

Sometimes a little mockery is exactly what it takes to get us going. Maybe we ought to count mockery as a blessing!

The second reason it was a blessing is because it gave the Jews time to get the wall built. The enemy underestimated them. If they had attacked immediately, humanly speaking, the Jews had no chance to defend themselves. But because they spent a good while mocking instead of going to battle against them right away, when they did choose to go to war against them, it was too late. Many times the things that we despise are actually blessings from the hand of our all-knowing God.

Look at how they worried and mocked them. Sanballat went first:

Nehemiah 4:2 *And he spake before his brethren and the army of Samaria, and said, What do these feeble Jews? will they fortify themselves? will they sacrifice? will they make an end in a day? will they revive the stones out of the heaps of the rubbish which are burned?*

Notice that he said what he said before an audience. The one who mocks God's people will always be seeking for an audience, whether it be a news program, or congress, or some Hollywood awards show. In this case, he said what he said in front of his brethren and in front of his army. This demonstrates what we noted a moment ago, they had the ability to attack immediately but did not. Their mocking actually gave the Jews time to get themselves into a defensible position.

His mockery was in the form of five questions.

The first question was a mockery of their ability. *What do these feeble Jews?* "You people are weak, you have no strength and ability, just go ahead and quit!"

42

By the way, can you hear the devil in that? How many times has he said that to a child of God? How many times has he said that to a preacher especially? And if we are not careful, we will fall into a "pious trap" that goes something like this, "Oh, you're right, I'm nothing, and I really can't do anything." That may sound good, but it ignores something very important:

Philippians 4:13 *I can do all things through Christ which strengtheneth me.*

Paul did not say, "I can't do anything, so I will just humbly wait for God to do something." No, he said, "God already has done something, He has strengthened me, and I can do anything." God's men from time to time could stand to have, not sinful pride, but a Holy Ghost empowered confidence about them that says, "Do not mess with me. God has strengthened me, and it is not going to go very well for you if you make an enemy out of me."

The second question was a mockery of their intelligence. *Will they fortify themselves?* "They think they have enough smarts to build up a defense system. They are way too dumb for that!"

The third question was a mockery of their devotion. *Will they sacrifice?* "Do they actually think that their religion or their God can help them?"

The fourth question was a mockery of their persistence. *Will they make an end in a day?* "It is going to take way longer than they think; they will give up before it is ever done."

The fifth question was a mockery of their situation. *Will they revive the stones out of the heaps of the rubbish which are burned?* "The task is too big. Too much damage has been done; they will never recover."

And when Sanballat was done, Tobiah jumped in with mockery of his own:

Nehemiah 4:3 *Now Tobiah the Ammonite was by him, and he said, Even that which they build, if a fox go up, he shall even break down their stone wall.*

A fox is a small animal, at its best maybe twenty pounds. Tobiah said, "Let them build, no worries, it will be such a pitiful wall that it will break apart the next time a little fox walks across it." People may not realize it, but one of the best things that can ever happen to you is for people to underestimate you. Never be upset about that, recognize it as a gift. If they underestimate you, they will not cause you nearly as many problems. How should you respond in the face of this type of mockery? Observe how Nehemiah responded:

Nehemiah 4:4 *Hear, O our God; for we are despised: and turn their reproach upon their own head, and give them for a prey in the land of captivity:* **5** *And cover not their iniquity, and let not their sin be blotted out from before thee: for they have provoked thee to anger before the builders.*

This is called an "imprecatory prayer." There are a great number of these in the Psalms, but they are also found throughout the rest of the Bible, including in the book of the Revelation where we see souls in Heaven praying one:

Revelation 6:9 *And when he had opened the fifth seal, I saw under the altar the souls of them that were slain for the word of God, and for the testimony which they held:* **10** *And they cried with a loud voice, saying, How long, O Lord, holy and true, dost thou not judge and avenge our blood on them that dwell on the earth?*

This is a prayer that God will hammer the enemies and not show them any mercy. Many people say that prayers of this nature were "for another dispensation." I do not believe that for a second. God has already promised throughout His Word to deal with the wicked; I see nothing wrong with praying for Him to do what He already said He would do.

Please notice the basis for him praying this. It was because *they have provoked **thee** to anger before the builders.* In other words, they did not just anger God, they did so in such a way as to discourage those who were laying it all on the line to serve Him. God is the best employer in the universe, and it angers Him greatly when His servants are despised and discouraged. That is why He gives us the right to walk into the big corner office, point out the offenders, and ask Him to deal with them.

The Workers

Nehemiah 4:6 *So built we the wall; and all the wall was joined together unto the half thereof: for the people had a mind to work.*

In a very short period of time, the entire wall was joined together and was at half of its intended height. This was a huge, enormous project. They had no heavy equipment, no dump trucks, no bulldozers, no cranes. Everything was done by hand. As far as the enemy could see, they were right in their ridicule. There was nothing that the Jews had that the enemy could see that would allow them to complete such a project. But there was one thing they had that the enemy could not see that more than made up for the things that they did not have: a mind to work.

May I say something? A **mind to work** is really more important than a **working mind**. In other words, effort is more important than intelligence. **Both are important**, but one is actually more important than the other. You can be a genius, a Ph.D, speak multiple languages, have a photographic memory, and if you are lazy none of that will do you a bit of good. But on the other hand you can have the intelligence of a broad-leaf weed, and if you will buckle down and go to work you will get more done than the lazy genius ever will.

Keep that thought in mind, we will come back to it.

The Warriors

Nehemiah 4:7 *But it came to pass, that when Sanballat, and Tobiah, and the Arabians, and the Ammonites, and the Ashdodites, heard that the walls of Jerusalem were made up, and that the breaches began to be stopped, then they were very wroth, 8 And conspired all of them together to come and to fight against Jerusalem, and to hinder it.*

This verse presents us something to be aware of. When enemies have begun to gather, they are a lot like rabbits in that they tend to multiply pretty quickly. We have already heard of Sanballat and Tobiah and Geshem, the Arabians and the Ammonites. Now we find the Ashdodites thrown into the mix. Ashdod was one of the five chief cities of the Philistines.

When these enemies heard that the wall was proceeding well, they banded together and formed a conspiracy, getting ready to move against the Jews militarily.

Nehemiah 4:9 *Nevertheless we made our prayer unto our God, and set a watch against them day and night, because of them.*

I find a fascinating set of words in this verse, the words "prayer" and "watch." We find them together several other times in Scripture:

Matthew 26:41 *Watch and pray, that ye enter not into temptation: the spirit indeed is willing, but the flesh is weak.*

Mark 13:33 *Take ye heed, watch and pray: for ye know not when the time is.*

Mark 14:38 *Watch ye and pray, lest ye enter into temptation. The spirit truly is ready, but the flesh is weak.*

Luke 21:36 *Watch ye therefore, and pray always, that ye may be accounted worthy to escape all these things that shall come to pass, and to stand before the Son of man.*

Four times Jesus told us not just to pray, but also to watch. The exact same combination Nehemiah used. We find a similar admonition using different wording in the book of Proverbs:

Proverbs 21:31 *The horse is prepared against the day of battle: but safety is of the LORD.*

Both sides must be present. We must pray, but we must also watch. We must know that safety is of the Lord, but we must also prepare the horse unto the day of battle. One is never complete without the other. Prayers need wings, but they also need feet. We need to trust; we also need to try. Nehemiah prayed **and** set a watch. He trusted God fully **and** also gave maximum effort.

Nehemiah 4:10 *And Judah said, The strength of the bearers of burdens is decayed, and there is much rubbish; so that we are not able to build the wall.*

Beginning in verse ten, three straight sources of discouragement are dropped into Nehemiah's lap. To begin with, we find those from the tribe of Judah coming to him with a two-part complaint. There were some people whose task it was to carry away the rubbish from the old wall and from the materials employed in building the new wall. Those people were exhausted. They believed they could not carry off even one more block. Because of that and the amount of rubbish left to move, they had reached a point where the building project had come to a standstill.

Then came the second source of discouragement:

Nehemiah 4:11 *And our adversaries said, They shall not know, neither see, till we come in the midst among them, and slay them, and cause the work to cease.*

Word came to Nehemiah of what his enemies were saying. They were saying that they were going to slip in among them secretly and kill them. That is almost worse than a frontal assault. The enemy you cannot see is worse than the one you can, because you always imagine the worst.

And then came the third source of discouragement:

Nehemiah 4:12 *And it came to pass, that when the Jews which dwelt by them came, they said unto us ten times, From all places whence ye shall return unto us they will be upon you.*

This was word from the Jews round about Jerusalem. They had it from "reliable yet anonymous sources" that people coming and going were going to be attacked, no matter which way they came or went. And they repeated that ten times! Now let me tell you what I find interesting. Look not just at what complaints Nehemiah answers, and how, but at which one he does not answer:

Nehemiah 4:13 *Therefore set I in the lower places behind the wall, and on the higher places, I even set the people after their families with their swords, their spears, and their bows.* **14** *And I looked, and rose up, and said unto the nobles, and to the rulers, and to the rest of the people, Be not ye afraid of them: remember the Lord, which is great and terrible, and fight for your brethren, your sons, and your daughters, your wives, and your houses.*

Nehemiah addressed the security issues. He put warriors in place, he put weapons in place, and he motivated them to fight. So which part did he not address? He did not address the part about the workers being too tired to remove the rubbish, and there being way too much rubbish to remove. He did not give a flowery speech, he did not come up with a brilliant plan. What did he do?

Nehemiah 4:15 *And it came to pass, when our enemies heard that it was known unto us, and God had brought their counsel to nought, that we returned all of us to the wall, every one unto his work.*

The enemy got word that the Jews were ready for any surprise attack. What did the Jews do? They simply got back to work. What was the solution to those who said, "We have way too many blocks to move; we can't do it?" The solution was to go back out there and move a few more blocks.

When we built our church building, it took 2½ years. We used 1,400 sheets of twelve- foot, 5/8 inch drywall. A lady from the Shelby Star interviewed me when we were done and asked if I ever felt like we would never get it done. I said, "No, ma'am. I knew that there were a definite, finite number of things to do in the project, and I reasoned that if I simply did a few more things every single day, eventually we would reach a point where there was nothing left to do."

There is one good solution to the problem of having an overwhelming task in front of you. Go pick up a few more blocks, then do the same thing tomorrow, and the day after that, and the day after that...

Nehemiah 4:16 *And it came to pass from that time forth, that the half of my servants wrought in the work, and the other half of them held both the spears, the shields, and the bows, and the habergeons; and the rulers were behind all the house of Judah.* **17** *They which builded on the wall, and they that bare burdens, with those that laded, every one with one of his hands wrought in the work, and with the other hand held a weapon.* **18** *For the builders, every one had his sword girded by his side, and so builded. And he that sounded the trumpet was by me.*

Nehemiah got everyone involved in both work and warfare at the exact same time. In fact, some groups of them had a tool in one hand and a sword in the other! Do you realize how hard it would be to work that way? But on the other hand, do you realize how unlikely an enemy would be to attack such a person? Do you really want to mess with someone who has a chainsaw in one hand and a sawed off shotgun in the other?

That would definitely be a person to leave alone. I believe that is exactly what Nehemiah had in mind. It would seem insane to anyone watching, insane enough to be dangerous.

Nehemiah 4:19 *And I said unto the nobles, and to the rulers, and to the rest of the people, The work is great and large, and we are separated upon the wall, one far from another.* **20** *In what place therefore ye hear the sound of the trumpet, resort ye thither unto us: our God shall fight for us.*

This sounds very much like the state of Bible believing churches today. The work is great and large, and we are separated far from each other. That being the case, we should be very vigilant to "come running when we hear the trumpet blow." We are very, very independent. So much so that I think we forget how badly we need each other:

Ecclesiastes 4:12 *And if one prevail against him, two shall withstand him; and a threefold cord is not quickly broken.*

Nehemiah 4:21 *So we laboured in the work: and half of them held the spears from the rising of the morning till the stars appeared.*

From morning until night. God bless workers with that type of heart!

Nehemiah 4:22 *Likewise at the same time said I unto the people, Let every one with his servant lodge within Jerusalem, that in the night they may be a guard to us, and labour on the day.*

Nehemiah tended to show great wisdom in everything he did, including this. The people from the countryside were used to going home after each day of work. He now stopped them and had everyone stay inside the city walls for protection. When you can convince people of the danger they face, you are doing something!

Nehemiah 4:23 *So neither I, nor my brethren, nor my servants, nor the men of the guard which followed me, none of us put off our clothes, saving that every one put them off for washing.*

This shows how serious they were about the task at hand. They slept in their clothing. They worked in their clothing. They kept the same things on for days and days and days until they just had to stop and wash them, then they did it all over again. Comfort was irrelevant, there was a job to do.

Coming back to the main thought of this chapter, the people had a mind to work. May I put it in my own words? There is no substitute for sweat. The Jews knew this. Every Jewish Rabbi taught his son a trade. They all memorized this quote: "If you do not teach your son a trade, you teach him to be a thief." One of my favorite news stories is this one:

Man leaves $50,000, car to waitress

Fri Dec 28, 2009 8:22 PM ET, associated press, Yahoo! News.

For nearly seven years Melina Salazar did her best to put on a smile and tend to the every need of her most loyal and cantankerous customer.

She made sure his food was as hot as he wanted, even if it meant he burned his mouth. And she smiled through his demands and curses. The 89-year-old Walter "Buck" Swords obviously appreciated it, leaving the waitress $50,000 and a 2000 Buick when he died.

"I still can't believe it," the Luby's Cafeteria employee told Harlingen television station KGBT-TV in an interview during which she described Swords as "kind of mean."

Swords, a World War II veteran, died in July. But Salazar learned just a few days before Christmas that he had left her the money and car.

Man honors hard work and so does God. He allowed Nehemiah and company to be successful not because they had "working minds," but because they had "minds to work."

Chapter Five
The Wrong Time to Turn a Profit

Nehemiah 5:1 And there was a great cry of the people and of their wives against their brethren the Jews. 2 For there were that said, We, our sons, and our daughters, are many: therefore we take up corn for them, that we may eat, and live. 3 Some also there were that said, We have mortgaged our lands, vineyards, and houses, that we might buy corn, because of the dearth. 4 There were also that said, We have borrowed money for the king's tribute, and that upon our lands and vineyards. 5 Yet now our flesh is as the flesh of our brethren, our children as their children: and, lo, we bring into bondage our sons and our daughters to be servants, and some of our daughters are brought unto bondage already: neither is it in our power to redeem them; for other men have our lands and vineyards. 6 And I was very angry when I heard their cry and these words. 7 Then I consulted with myself, and I rebuked the nobles, and the rulers, and said unto them, Ye exact usury, every one of his brother. And I set a great assembly against them. 8 And I said unto them, We after our ability have redeemed our brethren the Jews, which were sold unto the heathen; and will ye even sell your brethren? or shall they be sold unto us? Then held they their peace, and found nothing to answer. 9 Also I said, It is not good that ye do: ought ye not to walk in the fear of our God because of the reproach of the heathen our enemies? **10** *I likewise, and my brethren, and my servants, might exact of them money and corn: I pray you, let us leave off this usury.* **11** *Restore, I pray you, to them, even this day, their lands, their vineyards, their oliveyards, and their houses, also the hundredth part of the money, and of the corn, the wine, and the oil, that ye exact of them.* **12** *Then said they, We will restore them, and will require nothing of them; so will we do as thou sayest. Then I called the priests, and took an oath of them, that they should do according to this promise.* **13** *Also I shook my lap, and said, So God shake out every man from his house, and from his labour, that performeth not this promise, even thus be he shaken out, and emptied. And all the congregation said, Amen, and praised the LORD. And the people did according to this promise.* **14** *Moreover from the time that I was appointed to be their governor in the land of Judah, from the twentieth year even unto the two and thirtieth year of Artaxerxes the king, that is, twelve years, I and my brethren have not eaten the bread of the governor.* **15** *But the former governors that had been before me were chargeable unto the people, and had taken of them bread and wine, beside forty shekels of silver; yea, even their servants bare rule over the people: but so did not I, because of the fear of God.* **16** *Yea, also I continued in the work of this wall, neither bought we any land: and all my servants were gathered thither unto the work.* **17** *Moreover there were at my table an hundred and fifty of the Jews and rulers, beside those that came unto us from among the heathen that are about us.* **18** *Now that which was prepared for me daily was one ox and six choice sheep; also fowls were prepared for me, and once in ten days store of all sorts of wine: yet for all this required not I the bread of the governor, because the bondage was heavy upon this people.* **19** *Think upon me, my God, for good, according to all that I have done for this people.*

These days we are being told that people who make a profit are evil and need to be punished. But the capitalistic system, the system America has always operated under, is both right and Biblical. The system where people are expected to work, save, and be smart with their money is right. The system where people who take great personal risks to achieve great things and end up becoming wealthy because of it is right. A person who invests his life savings, risks losing everything, works 90 hours a week to start his own company, and sees that company grow into a multi-billion dollar corporation ought to be rewarded far more than the person who simply works a 9 to 5 job with no risk to themselves or their own money.

Profit is not a sinful thing. However, there are actually times when we should intentionally not make a profit! There are times when we should be trying to either break even or actually show a loss. Those times are *rare,* but they do exist. The Jews in Nehemiah's day found themselves in one of those situations, and Nehemiah had to teach them what they were doing wrong.

The Problem

The first four chapters introduced us to the first part of the problem. These people had just come back from captivity. The walls were destroyed, the city burned, and they all had to spend their days trying to fix it. There were enemies all around threatening to destroy them. So in addition to having to work on the walls all day, they were also having to hold swords and weapons and stand guard all day and night lest they be overrun. In a time like that, you do not have much of an opportunity to provide for even the basic needs of you and your family. It was a time of great emergency, these people were just trying to stay alive. Chapter five then introduces us to two more parts of the problem:

Nehemiah 5:1 *And there was a great cry of the people and of their wives against their brethren the Jews. 2 For there were that said, We, our sons, and our daughters, are many: therefore we take up corn for them, that we may eat, and live. 3 Some also there were that said, We have mortgaged our lands, vineyards, and houses, that we might buy corn, because of the dearth. 4 There were also that said, We have borrowed money for the king's tribute, and that upon our lands and vineyards. 5 Yet now our flesh is as the flesh of our brethren, our children as their children: and, lo, we bring into bondage our sons and our daughters to be servants, and some of our daughters are brought unto bondage already: neither is it in our power to redeem them; for other men have our lands and vineyards.*

In addition to everything else they were facing, the rains were not coming. It was a time of dearth; they were in a famine. That is bad timing! But on top of that, they were under a huge tax burden. They were actually having to borrow money to pay their taxes.

The Profit

When these hard times hit, some better off people saw what they believed was a good opportunity to make a profit:

Nehemiah 5:1 *And there was a great cry of the people and of their wives against their brethren the Jews.*

At the very outset, we find that the people who found a great way to make money off of people in desperate times were their own brethren, the other Jews. This was not a case of being gouged by strangers; this was family gouging family!

Nehemiah 5:2 *For there were that said, We, our sons, and our daughters, are many: therefore we take up corn for them, that we may eat, and live.*

The phrase *take up corn for them* means that they borrowed money to get corn. They had big families and were going to "finance companies" with high interest rates just to buy food. They were being destroyed financially, but their brethren were making a very nice profit off of them.

Nehemiah 5:3 *Some also there were that said, We have mortgaged our lands, vineyards, and houses, that we might buy corn, because of the dearth.*

This group of people actually mortgaged their houses and lands and farms just to buy food. That means they had nowhere to live and nowhere to work. They were being destroyed, but their brethren were making a healthy profit off of them.

Nehemiah 5:4 *There were also that said, We have borrowed money for the king's tribute, and that upon our lands and vineyards.*

These people were having to borrow money to pay their taxes in order to keep their lands, and once again, their brethren were making a killing off of them.

Nehemiah 5:5 *Yet now our flesh is as the flesh of our brethren, our children as their children: and, lo, we bring into* *bondage our sons and our daughters to be servants, and some of our daughters are brought unto bondage already: neither is it in our power to redeem them; for other men have our lands and vineyards.*

Our flesh is as the flesh of our brethren, our children as their children. They were saying "We are all humans, all made in the image of God, and all Israelites. We all worship the same God, we all are working on the same walls, we all have the same enemies." These people should have had enough of a sense of camaraderie about them to not regard a time of disaster and distress as a money-making opportunity! The law of Moses allowed people under extreme circumstances of poverty to put their own children under bondage to some businessman to pay their debts. These people, who were working like dogs for one another trying to build a wall so that everyone, rich and poor alike could survive, were having to sell their own children into bondage. Some of the daughters had already been sold, breaking their parent's hearts. The law allowed them to raise the money and buy them back at any time, but they had no money and no way to make any money since the creditors had already taken their lands.

But who cares if people have worked like dogs to build walls for everyone, rich and poor, just so they could all survive? Who cares if people have seen their crops dry up because of the dearth? Who cares if the government has put such a high tax on people that they are losing everything and having to take out loans just to pay the taxes? Who cares if it has gotten so bad that people are having to sell their own children into bondage? Times like that are a golden money-making opportunity!

How wicked! Most of the time it is fine and dandy to make a profit, but in times like that, who in their right minds, who with any type of a heart could treat his own brethren like that? We are not talking about normal times. We are not even talking about people like most people are today, who confuse luxuries with necessities. We are not talking about people who have been foolish and ought to be made to pay the price for their folly. Matthew Henry said:

"If men borrow large sums to trade with, to increase their stocks, or to purchase land, there is no reason why the lender should not share with the borrower in his profit; or if to spend upon their lusts, or repair what they have so spent, why should they not pay for their extravagances? But if the poor borrow to maintain their families, and we be able to help them, it is certain we ought either to lend freely what they have occasion for, or (if they be not likely to repay it) to give freely something towards it."

In other words, if people are trying to make money and they need you to give them a loan, or they need to hire you to do something, you have every right to make money off of it. If people want some luxury; a new deck, a paint job, a perm, a photo shoot, a TV, a patio, whatever, you ought to make money off of it. If people have been foolish and blown their money on drugs or drink or TVs or jewelry, and now they need money from you, you ought to make money off of them. But if your brethren are doing things right and end up in dire straits anyway and you have the ability to help them, cut them some slack! Do not look at them and see dollar signs; look at them and see Jesus. Help them as if they were Him.

Matthew 25:34 *Then shall the King say unto them on his right hand, Come, ye blessed of my Father, inherit the kingdom prepared for you from the foundation of the world:* **35** *For I was an hungred, and ye gave me meat: I was thirsty, and ye gave me drink: I was a stranger, and ye took me in:* **36** *Naked, and ye clothed me: I was sick, and ye visited me: I was in prison, and ye came unto me.* **37** *Then shall the righteous answer him, saying, Lord, when saw we thee an hungred, and fed thee? or thirsty, and gave thee drink?* **38** *When saw we thee a stranger, and took thee in? or naked, and clothed thee?* **39** *Or when saw we thee sick, or in prison, and came unto thee?* **40** *And the King shall answer and say unto them, Verily I say unto you, Inasmuch as ye have done it unto one of the least of these my brethren, ye have done it unto me.*

I see things that gall me on both ends of the spectrum. For instance, a hurricane comes through. People immediately raise the price of a bag of ice to $15.00. Then the government steps in and regulates prices and makes them give it away. Listen to me. The government has no business telling people what they can and cannot charge for anything. And the moment you give them that power, in *any* circumstance, they will feel free to use it in *every* circumstance. But at the same time people ought to have enough of a heart not to gouge people when they are hurting! It ought not take some government bureaucrat to make people do right; people ought to just do right. These Jews were slaving away all day every day trying to build the walls that would defend their rich brethren. They were working for free trying to build the walls that would defend their rich brethren. Yet their rich brethren were turning around and making a huge profit off of them in the midst of disaster!

The Payback

Nehemiah 5:6 *And I was very angry when I heard their cry and these words.* **7** *Then I consulted with myself, and I rebuked the nobles, and the rulers, and said unto them, Ye exact usury, every one of his brother. And I set a great assembly against them.*

When Nehemiah heard the cries of the hurting people, and when he realized what was going on, he was beside himself. So much so that he was able to *consult with himself!* He was so mad that he was talking to himself. He did not assemble a committee to investigate the problem; the problem was clear. He consulted with himself, then he chewed out the guilty parties.

That all by itself shows a great deal about the character of Nehemiah. These men that he was chewing out were the "money men" in the city!

Some in church are able to give more than others. That does not mean they ought to have any more influence than anyone else. In our church, we do not yet have that problem/blessing. Everyone who actually tithes is pretty close in what they give to what everyone else gives. No one at Cornerstone is rich. But if any of you ever get to the point where you are giving way more than anyone else, please remember that your opinion is still worth just exactly as much and just exactly as little as anyone else who is tithing. And you who may one day be pastors, you need to remember never to treat any big givers any better, or any worse, than anyone else.

The accusation that Nehemiah leveled against them was that they were "exacting usury" against their brethren. Usury means interest. The Jews had a very specific law on this:

Deuteronomy 23:19 *Thou shalt not lend upon usury to thy brother; usury of money, usury of victuals, usury of any thing that is lent upon usury:* **20** *Unto a stranger thou mayest lend upon usury; but unto thy brother thou shalt not lend upon usury: that the LORD thy God may bless thee in all that thou settest thine hand to in the land whither thou goest to possess it.*

Interest was not forbidden.

Matthew 25:27 *Thou oughtest therefore to have put my money to the exchangers, and then at my coming I should have received mine own with usury.*

But charging it to brethren, especially poor brethren, was. Remember, we are now talking about interest, not profit off of a product or service. Do not think that it is wrong to make a profit off of goods or services. Under most circumstances, that is perfectly fine. But these Jews in the days of Nehemiah were not doing that. They were making a profit by charging interest on loans to poor brethren who were slaving away for free building a wall that would keep those rich money lenders and everyone else safe. They were profiting off of charging interest in a time of distress and disaster, when everyone should have been pulling together.

Nehemiah, after he pointed these things out, *set a great assembly against them.* There were a ton of witnesses to all that was happening. Now, Nehemiah himself was rich. So here was a rich man chewing out other rich men. Did he have any moral right to do so? In other words, was he in any way being hypocritical? Not even close. Look at the next verse:

Nehemiah 5:8 *And I said unto them, We after our ability have redeemed our brethren the Jews, which were sold unto the heathen; and will ye even sell your brethren? or shall they be sold unto us? Then held they their peace, and found nothing to answer.*

Nehemiah and some others had been spending their own money to redeem other Jews who had been sold into bondage, while these other rich Jews were busy making a profit selling their brethren into bondage. Nehemiah said: "Should you be doing that? Do you maybe even expect us to be your customers, to buy people from you, when we are spending our own money to get people out of bondage?"

They could not think of a thing to say to that. That is good, that is very good. Sometimes people just need to be quiet and take their medicine.

Nehemiah 5:9 *Also I said, It is not good that ye do: ought ye not to walk in the fear of our God because of the reproach of the heathen our enemies?*

The enemies were watching the Jews, looking for something wrong. The Jews claimed to be people of God, so, like always, the devil's crowd was looking for anything they could accuse them with. And they were giving it to them!

Nehemiah 5:10 *I likewise, and my brethren, and my servants, might exact of them money and corn: I pray you, let us leave off this usury.* **11** *Restore, I pray you, to them, even this day, their lands, their vineyards, their oliveyards, and their houses, also the hundredth part of the money, and of the corn, the wine, and the oil, that ye exact of them.*

Nehemiah pointed out that he and his crowd could be doing the exact same thing. They could be making a killing off of charging interest to hurting people, but they were not. He then said, publically, "Why don't you guys give that money back, and whatever else you have gotten from them?" He mentioned the one hundredth part of the money. Interest was normally done each month, so this lets us know that they were charging 12% annual interest. 12% interest to poor brethren, in a dearth, under heavy taxation, working for free, building a wall to defend the city. That is incredibly inappropriate.

Nehemiah 5:12 *Then said they, We will restore them, and will require nothing of them; so will we do as thou sayest. Then I called the priests, and took an oath of them, that they should do according to this promise.* **13** *Also I shook my lap, and said, So God shake out every man from his house, and from his labour, that performeth not this promise, even thus be he shaken* *out, and emptied. And all the congregation said, Amen, and praised the LORD. And the people did according to this promise.*

Let's give credit where it is due. I really admire the fact that these men were willing to see and admit the error of their ways and fix things. That takes a big person.

Nehemiah shook the robe on his lap, shaking out the dust and debris, and said, "Ok, you have promised. If you do not follow through, God is going to shake you out of His lap like crumbs onto the ground."

The Pattern

Nehemiah 5:14 *Moreover from the time that I was appointed to be their governor in the land of Judah, from the twentieth year even unto the two and thirtieth year of Artaxerxes the king, that is, twelve years, I and my brethren have not eaten the bread of the governor. **15** But the former governors that had been before me were chargeable unto the people, and had taken of them bread and wine, beside forty shekels of silver; yea, even their servants bare rule over the people: but so did not I, because of the fear of God.*

The *bread of the governor* Nehemiah referred to was a rather luxurious salary of daily bread and wine and forty shekels of silver. That was a high-dollar salary, especially considering how badly things were going in the country economically. The people that were governors before Nehemiah took that full salary and even put their servants in ruling positions over the people.

Nehemiah did not. He refused to even take a salary for twelve years of work! He lived off of his own savings and did not take a salary. That made what the rich money lenders were doing even more scandalous by comparison.

Nehemiah was setting a pattern of right doing for the people to follow.

By the way, I find an interesting parallel in our modern day. Government, the President, our Congress, every day go on television and bash the CEO's of banks and companies for taking huge salaries while their companies do poorly and rack up enormous debts. But no organization on earth is racking up more debt than the United States government at all levels. The debt they are racking up is our money, not theirs, and yet they are still, every one of them, taking their huge enormous salaries and their life-long benefits packages. They keep on saying that CEO's should be put on merit pay and only make money if they perform well. I think Congress and the President should be put on merit pay and only get paid if *they* perform well!

Nehemiah did not just tell people how they should behave, he showed people how to behave. Look at an even further description of that:

Nehemiah 5:16 *Yea, also I continued in the work of this wall, neither bought we any land: and all my servants were gathered thither unto the work.*

Nehemiah could have made a killing in real estate by buying land dirt-cheap from hurting people, but he did not. Those hurting people were not strangers; they were brethren who were working on the wall. So Nehemiah spent his days actually physically working on the walls alongside them, and his servants did too.

Nehemiah 5:17 *Moreover there were at my table an hundred and fifty of the Jews and rulers, beside those that came unto us from among the heathen that are about us.* **18** *Now that which was prepared for me daily was one ox and six choice sheep; also fowls were prepared for me, and once in ten days store of all sorts of wine: yet for all this required not I the bread of the governor, because the bondage was heavy upon this people.*

Every day Nehemiah personally fed more than 150 of the Jews at his own table, at his own expense. Every day he shelled out his own money for one ox, six choice sheep, all kinds of birds, and every ten days a bunch of wine. But in spite of all of that expense he still did not take the salary due to him as the governor, because the people were hurting so bad and struggling so hard.

How can a person make it while not taking what is "owed" them? How can people make it without charging interest to hurting brethren? Under normal circumstances, God will provide for us by the profits He allows us to make in business, either as an owner or as an employee. Under devastatingly hard circumstances, God will provide for us in spite of the profits we do not make and the interest we do not charge.

Nehemiah 5:19 *Think upon me, my God, for good, according to all that I have done for this people.*

If Nehemiah was there for twelve years as governor with no salary and charging no interest and did not starve, it certainly appears that God took quite good care of him. There is a right time to make a profit and a wrong time to make a profit.

Chapter Six
Satan's Subtle Strategies

Nehemiah 6:1 *Now it came to pass, when Sanballat, and Tobiah, and Geshem the Arabian, and the rest of our enemies, heard that I had builded the wall, and that there was no breach left therein; (though at that time I had not set up the doors upon the gates;) 2 That Sanballat and Geshem sent unto me, saying, Come, let us meet together in some one of the villages in the plain of Ono. But they thought to do me mischief. 3 And I sent messengers unto them, saying, I am doing a great work, so that I cannot come down: why should the work cease, whilst I leave it, and come down to you? 4 Yet they sent unto me four times after this sort; and I answered them after the same manner. 5 Then sent Sanballat his servant unto me in like manner the fifth time with an open letter in his hand; 6 Wherein was written, It is reported among the heathen, and Gashmu saith it, that thou and the Jews think to rebel: for which cause thou buildest the wall, that thou mayest be their king, according to these words. 7 And thou hast also appointed prophets to preach of thee at Jerusalem, saying, There is a king in Judah: and now shall it be reported to the king according to these words. Come now therefore, and let us take counsel together. 8 Then I sent unto him, saying, There are no such things done as thou sayest, but thou feignest them out of thine own heart. 9 For they all made us afraid, saying, Their hands shall be weakened from the work, that it be not done. Now therefore, O God, strengthen my hands.*

10 Afterward I came unto the house of Shemaiah the son of Delaiah the son of Mehetabeel, who was shut up; and he said, Let us meet together in the house of God, within the temple, and let us shut the doors of the temple: for they will come to slay thee; yea, in the night will they come to slay thee. 11 And I said, Should such a man as I flee? and who is there, that, being as I am, would go into the temple to save his life? I will not go in. 12 And, lo, I perceived that God had not sent him; but that he pronounced this prophecy against me: for Tobiah and Sanballat had hired him. 13 Therefore was he hired, that I should be afraid, and do so, and sin, and that they might have matter for an evil report, that they might reproach me. 14 My God, think thou upon Tobiah and Sanballat according to these their works, and on the prophetess Noadiah, and the rest of the prophets, that would have put me in fear. 15 So the wall was finished in the twenty and fifth day of the month Elul, in fifty and two days. 16 And it came to pass, that when all our enemies heard thereof, and all the heathen that were about us saw these things, they were much cast down in their own eyes: for they perceived that this work was wrought of our God. 17 Moreover in those days the nobles of Judah sent many letters unto Tobiah, and the letters of Tobiah came unto them. 18 For there were many in Judah sworn unto him, because he was the son in law of Shechaniah the son of Arah; and his son Johanan had taken the daughter of Meshullam the son of Berechiah. 19 Also they reported his good deeds before me, and uttered my words to him. And Tobiah sent letters to put me in fear.

In chapter four we found that the people had a mind to work, even if it meant holding a weapon in one hand and a tool in the other. By the time chapter four was done the wall was joined together all the way around and was at half of its intended height.

In chapter five Nehemiah had to take time and deal with internal problems. These people who had come back out of bondage were enslaving each other. They were charging each other insanely high interest on loans; they were treating each other like the heathens had treated them. Nehemiah led the way in showing everyone how to treat everyone else like they were supposed to.

That brings us to chapter six, when our attention will again be brought back to the enemies from without. This time they will be much more subtle than before. What they could not accomplish by threats they will now try to accomplish with trickery.

Destruction through Diplomacy

Nehemiah 6:1 *Now it came to pass, when Sanballat, and Tobiah, and Geshem the Arabian, and the rest of our enemies, heard that I had builded the wall, and that there was no breach left therein; (though at that time I had not set up the doors upon the gates;)* **2** *That Sanballat and Geshem sent unto me, saying, Come, let us meet together in some one of the villages in the plain of Ono. But they thought to do me mischief.*

The means used to stop the building of the wall had failed miserably. So, turning to more subtle means, the enemies of the work sent a message to Nehemiah that they would like to meet with him. "Meet" means "assemble," as in "sit down and have some diplomacy." And where did they desire for this diplomacy to take place? In perhaps the most ironic sounding of places, the plain of Ono!

We may learn some valuable things from this attack and attempt by the enemies of the work. We may first of all learn that "diplomacy" with your enemies is never intended to benefit you!

The story is told of a hunter that went into the woods to shoot a bear. When he found one to shoot, the bear said, "Let's sit down and talk about this. Put down your gun, then you tell me what you want, I'll tell you what I want, and we'll see if we can reach some diplomatic solution." The hunter said, "Great idea! I want a fur coat to wear." The bear said, "OK, I want a full belly. I think we can work something out." A few moments later, the bear left the woods alone, he had a full belly, and the hunter had a fur coat!

If you sit down to talk with the devil, he will eat you!

We should also learn that if people have been trying to destroy you and then suddenly become friendly when you have gotten successful, they are not really your friends!

Choose your friends very carefully and recognize your enemies as enemies even when they want you to have a diplomatic meeting with them!

Nehemiah 6:3 *And I sent messengers unto them, saying, I am doing a great work, so that I cannot come down: why should the work cease, whilst I leave it, and come down to you?* **4** *Yet they sent unto me four times after this sort; and I answered them after the same manner.*

This was the absolute truth; he was not "thinking of an excuse." We ought to always be doing "a great work!" And doing that great work should always be more important than catering to our enemies!

Notice also that Nehemiah was not worn down by the persistent requests. The enemies of the work sent to him four times trying to get this meeting arranged. What they could not accomplish by other means, they attempted to accomplish by pushing and pushing and pushing, hoping to wear Nehemiah down.

The first of *Satan's Subtle Strategies* was destruction by diplomacy.

Destruction through Feigned Concern

Nehemiah 6:5 *Then sent Sanballat his servant unto me in like manner the fifth time with an open letter in his hand;* **6** *Wherein was written, It is reported among the heathen, and Gashmu saith it, that thou and the Jews think to rebel: for which cause thou buildest the wall, that thou mayest be their king, according to these words.* **7** *And thou hast also appointed prophets to preach of thee at Jerusalem, saying, There is a king in Judah: and now shall it be reported to the king according to these words. Come now therefore, and let us take counsel together.*

Sanballat, dear, dear Sanballat, was so concerned about Nehemiah's reputation! The accusation was a serious one, namely that Nehemiah was building the wall so that he could lead the Jews in a rebellion against the King of Persia and become king himself over the Jews there in Israel. The thing is, this "concern" for Nehemiah was going to stop the work. That was the only clue Nehemiah needed to know the concern was not genuine. If the concern had been genuine Sanballat himself could have stopped all the talking, since he was the ring leader!

If people claim to be concerned over things they could stop, they are not really concerned:

Oh, pastor, people are telling me some pretty terrible things about you, and I am really concerned...

No, you are not. If you were really concerned, you would not be listening to them; you would be telling them to shut their mouths!

Oh, pastor, the ladies have been coming to me with some pretty nasty things to say about your wife, and I am really concerned...

No, you are not. If you were really concerned, when they started talking, you would immediately haul them to the pastor's wife and make them say it in front of her!

And by the way, Sanballat had more character than most accusers in most churches; he at least named the accuser! The most yellow-bellied, sissified, effeminate thing in this world is the anonymous complaint. Never, ever be guilty of listening to or repeating one!

Nehemiah 6:8 *Then I sent unto him, saying, There are no such things done as thou sayest, but thou feignest them out of thine own heart.* **9** *For they all made us afraid, saying, Their hands shall be weakened from the work, that it be not done. Now therefore, O God, strengthen my hands.*

In verse eight you see a response that shows no fear. But in verse nine you see that Nehemiah actually was worried about this. The accusation was enough to get him killed! But Nehemiah was wise enough to show no fear in front of the enemy. What a leader shows outwardly, those who follow that leader will feel inwardly.

The first two of *Satan's Subtle Strategies* were destruction through diplomacy and destruction through feigned concern.

Destruction through Self-Preservation

Nehemiah 6:10 *Afterward I came unto the house of Shemaiah the son of Delaiah the son of Mehetabeel, who was shut up; and he said, Let us meet together in the house of God,* *within the temple, and let us shut the doors of the temple: for they will come to slay thee; yea, in the night will they come to slay thee.*

This was perhaps the most subtle attack of all. It came from the son of a priest; it came from within the house of God. The tactic was this: get Nehemiah to lock himself up in the house of God to secure his own safety. And do you know what? It would have worked. Nehemiah would have been safe locked up behind the walls and shut doors of God's house. The enemy would not have bothered him, because he would not have been bothering the enemy!

The devil would love for every one of us to take that option. Just give him the entire world, and he will let us lock ourselves and a few old people inside the walls of the church until we all die off and go away. We will have been safe all the way to the grave, and we will have wasted our entire lives along the way and done nothing at all for God.

Would you like a list of some things it would be safer not to do? Bus ministries, tracts handed out, soul-winning, camps, radio ministries, preaching against the prevailing sins of the day...

But we are not in this thing for safety's sake!

Nehemiah 6:11 *And I said, Should such a man as I flee? and who is there, that, being as I am, would go into the temple to save his life? I will not go in.*

Nehemiah understood something. God puts some people out front to take the arrows so that the people behind will have the courage to follow. It is never the arrows from out front that stop such a man but the knives from the back!

Nehemiah 6:12 *And, lo, I perceived that God had not sent him; but that he pronounced this prophecy against me: for Tobiah and Sanballat had hired him.* **13** *Therefore was he hired, that I should be afraid, and do so, and sin, and that they might have matter for an evil report, that they might reproach me.* **14** *My God, think thou upon Tobiah and Sanballat according to these their works, and on the prophetess Noadiah, and the rest of the prophets, that would have put me in fear.*

Nothing else was said, but after Shemaiah said what he said Nehemiah *perceived that God had not sent him.* In other words, he read the guy's face when he answered him. He figured out in a flash that he was a "bought" preacher, and that the enemy was writing the checks!

Verse fourteen singles out a "her" like the "him;" a woman named Noadiah. This points out for us that both men and women are capable of being employed by the enemy.

The first three of *Satan's Subtle Strategies* were destruction through diplomacy, destruction through feigned concern, and destruction through self-preservation.

Destruction through Wrong Loyalties

Nehemiah 6:15 *So the wall was finished in the twenty and fifth day of the month Elul, in fifty and two days.*

This was an amazing accomplishment! From a busted down wall laying in heaps of rubble, Nehemiah rallied the people, moved the rubble, and rebuilt the entire wall of the city in fifty-two days. With no power equipment, hydraulic tools, or diesel engines, working only by hand, they accomplished the task and did so with amazing speed.

Nehemiah 6:16 *And it came to pass, that when all our enemies heard thereof, and all the heathen that were about us saw these things, they were much cast down in their own eyes: for they perceived that this work was wrought of our God.*

There is an old song titled "My Favorite Things." Well this is one of my favorite things: when enemies who make it their business to make a church and a pastor miserable end up being miserable over the happiness of that church and pastor! Refuse to drag your bottom lip for people who want you to do so. Make it a point to be happy and to let people who want you to be unhappy know that you are happy!

The last tactic, wrong loyalties, begins to be shown in verse seventeen, and it is the one that angers me the most.

Nehemiah 6:17 *Moreover in those days the nobles of Judah sent many letters unto Tobiah, and the letters of Tobiah came unto them.*

Tobiah was the enemy. Tobiah was the enemy. Tobiah was the enemy! But he was friends with a lot of folks there, and even when he became an open enemy of God's work these people stayed friends with him. They "continued to correspond."

God's man and your church family are extremely important. They are important enough that, if a friend who is against them wants to "correspond with you," the answer ought to be no. People are foolish and inappropriate to write, call, e-mail, fellowship, or Facebook with people who do not like their pastor or their church.

You wives, how would you feel if your husband was to write, call, e-mail, fellowship, or Facebook with someone who does not like you?

Husbands, how would you feel if your wife was to write, call, e-mail, fellowship, or Facebook with someone who does not like you?

This is a big deal! People with just a wrong look on their face can change the way you feel about your pastor, his family, or your church.

Nehemiah 6:18 *For there were many in Judah sworn unto him, because he was the son in law of Shechaniah the son of Arah; and his son Johanan had taken the daughter of Meshullam the son of Berechiah.*

Those consorting with the enemy of the work were tied to this particular man because some of them were related to him. I have a newsflash for you: I would not even let my family bad-mouth my church, pastor, or church family. I cannot change the fact that I am related to them, but I do know how to tell them to keep their mouths shut!

Nehemiah 6:19 *Also they reported his good deeds before me, and uttered my words to him. And Tobiah sent letters to put me in fear.*

In other words, they told Nehemiah all about the successes of his enemy, and they told his enemy all of his secret counsels. They were building up Tobiah and tearing down Nehemiah. Now let this sink in: these people were in the city with Nehemiah! They were Jews! They were people that Nehemiah was sacrificing everything for to help and serve. Talk about unintelligent! How dumb must people be to stand against a man of God who is giving everything to help them? How dumb must they be to stand with his enemies?

Not much makes me furious, but through the years, this has more than once made me furious. We will love people and help people and pray for people and serve people. We will be there when they are in the hospital, we will be there when they are having troubles in the home, we will be there when a pipe has busted, we will be there when a heart is broken. And then despite all of that, there will be someone who used to go to church alongside us and got mad for some reason and runs their mouth about us, and people that we have done so much for just keep right on being friends with them like nothing is wrong!

If someone leaves right, on good terms, and does not try to tear the work down, be friends with them all you like. Not everybody needs to be at my church or at yours. But if someone is bashing the church, or giving those obnoxious facial expressions when the pastor is mentioned, or just giving those subtle insinuations that you might be better off at another church, have enough of a brain to cut them off completely. They are not trying to do you or us any favors.

Satan's strategies are subtle, but they are deadly!

Chapter Seven
The Genealogy

Nehemiah 7:1 *Now it came to pass, when the wall was built, and I had set up the doors, and the porters and the singers and the Levites were appointed,* **2** *That I gave my brother Hanani, and Hananiah the ruler of the palace, charge over Jerusalem: for he was a faithful man, and feared God above many.* **3** *And I said unto them, Let not the gates of Jerusalem be opened until the sun be hot; and while they stand by, let them shut the doors, and bar them: and appoint watches of the inhabitants of Jerusalem, every one in his watch, and every one to be over against his house.* **4** *Now the city was large and great: but the people were few therein, and the houses were not builded.* **5** *And my God put into mine heart to gather together the nobles, and the rulers, and the people, that they might be reckoned by genealogy. And I found a register of the genealogy of them which came up at the first, and found written therein,* **6** *These are the children of the province, that went up out of the captivity, of those that had been carried away, whom Nebuchadnezzar the king of Babylon had carried away, and came again to Jerusalem and to Judah, every one unto his city;* **7** *Who came with Zerubbabel, Jeshua, Nehemiah, Azariah, Raamiah, Nahamani, Mordecai, Bilshan, Mispereth, Bigvai, Nehum, Baanah. The number, I say, of the men of the people of Israel was this;* **8** *The children of Parosh, two thousand an hundred seventy and two.* **9** *The children of Shephatiah, three* *hundred seventy and two.* **10** *The children of Arah, six hundred fifty and two.* **11** *The children of Pahathmoab, of the children of Jeshua and Joab, two thousand and eight hundred and eighteen.* **12** *The children of Elam, a thousand two hundred fifty and four.* **13** *The children of Zattu, eight hundred forty and five.* **14** *The children of Zaccai, seven hundred and threescore.* **15** *The children of Binnui, six hundred forty and eight.* **16** *The children of Bebai, six hundred twenty and eight.* **17** *The children of Azgad, two thousand three hundred twenty and two.* **18** *The children of Adonikam, six hundred threescore and seven.* **19** *The children of Bigvai, two thousand threescore and seven.* **20** *The children of Adin, six hundred fifty and five.* **21** *The children of Ater of Hezekiah, ninety and eight.* **22** *The children of Hashum, three hundred twenty and eight.* **23** *The children of Bezai, three hundred twenty and four.* **24** *The children of Hariph, an hundred and twelve.* **25** *The children of Gibeon, ninety and five.* **26** *The men of Bethlehem and Netophah, an hundred fourscore and eight.* **27** The men of Anathoth, an hundred *twenty and eight.* **28** *The men of Bethazmaveth, forty and two.* **29** *The men of Kirjathjearim, Chephirah, and Beeroth, seven hundred forty and three.* **30** *The men of Ramah and Geba, six hundred twenty and one.* **31** *The men of Michmas, an hundred and twenty and two.* **32** *The men of Bethel and Ai, an hundred twenty and three.* **33** *The men of the other Nebo, fifty and two.* **34** *The children of the other Elam, a thousand two hundred fifty and four.* **35** *The children of Harim, three hundred and twenty.* **36** *The children of Jericho, three hundred forty and five.* **37** *The children of Lod, Hadid, and Ono, seven hundred twenty and one.* **38** *The children of Senaah, three thousand nine hundred and thirty.* **39** *The priests: the children of Jedaiah, of the house of Jeshua, nine hundred seventy and three.* **40** *The children of Immer, a thousand fifty and two.* **41** *The children of Pashur, a thousand two hundred forty and seven.* **42** *The children of Harim, a thousand and seventeen.* **43** *The Levites: the children of Jeshua, of Kadmiel, and of the children of Hodevah, seventy and four.* **44** *The singers: the children of Asaph, an hundred forty and eight.* **45** *The porters: the children of Shallum, the children of Ater, the children of Talmon, the children of Akkub, the children of Hatita, the children of Shobai, an hundred thirty and eight.* **46**

The Nethinims: the children of Ziha, the children of Hashupha, the children of Tabbaoth, **47** *The children of Keros, the children of Sia, the children of Padon,* **48** *The children of Lebana, the children of Hagaba, the children of Shalmai,* **49** *The children of Hanan, the children of Giddel, the children of Gahar,* **50** *The children of Reaiah, the children of Rezin, the children of Nekoda,* **51** *The children of Gazzam, the children of Uzza, the children of Phaseah,* **52** *The children of Besai, the children of Meunim, the children of Nephishesim,* **53** *The children of Bakbuk, the children of Hakupha, the children of Harhur,* **54** *The children of Bazlith, the children of Mehida, the children of Harsha,* **55** *The children of Barkos, the children of Sisera, the children of Tamah,* **56** *The children of Neziah, the children of Hatipha.* **57** *The children of Solomon's servants: the children of Sotai, the children of Sophereth, the children of Perida,* **58** *The children of Jaala, the children of Darkon, the children of Giddel,* **59** *The children of Shephatiah, the children of Hattil, the children of Pochereth of Zebaim, the children of Amon.* **60** *All the Nethinims, and the children of Solomon's servants, were three hundred ninety and two.* **61** *And these were they which went up also from Telmelah, Telharesha, Cherub, Addon, and Immer: but they could not shew their father's house, nor their seed, whether they were of Israel.* **62** *The children of Delaiah, the children of Tobiah, the children of Nekoda, six hundred forty and two.* **63** *And of the priests: the children of Habaiah, the children of Koz, the children of Barzillai, which took one of the daughters of Barzillai the Gileadite to wife, and was called after their name.* **64** *These sought their register among those that were reckoned by genealogy, but it was not found: therefore were they, as polluted, put from the priesthood.* **65** *And the Tirshatha said unto them, that they should not eat of the most holy things, till there stood up a priest with Urim and Thummim.* **66** *The whole congregation together was forty and two thousand three hundred and threescore,* **67** *Beside their manservants and their maidservants, of whom there were seven thousand three hundred thirty and seven: and they had two hundred forty and five singing men and singing women.* **68** *Their horses, seven hundred thirty and six: their mules, two hundred forty and five:* **69** *Their camels, four hundred thirty and five: six thousand* *seven hundred and twenty asses.* **70** *And some of the chief of the fathers gave unto the work. The Tirshatha gave to the treasure a thousand drams of gold, fifty basons, five hundred and thirty priests' garments.* **71** *And some of the chief of the fathers gave to the treasure of the work twenty thousand drams of gold, and two thousand and two hundred pound of silver.* **72** *And that which the rest of the people gave was twenty thousand drams of gold, and two thousand pound of silver, and threescore and seven priests' garments.* **73** *So the priests, and the Levites, and the porters, and the singers, and some of the people, and the Nethinims, and all Israel, dwelt in their cities; and when the seventh month came, the children of Israel were in their cities.*

In chapter one God moved on the heart of a man with a comfortable life and a comfortable job, a Jew by the name of Nehemiah. Nehemiah became burdened to rebuild the ravaged walls of Jerusalem. So in chapter two, after four months of praying, God had the king notice Nehemiah's sad countenance and ask him what was wrong. Nehemiah ended up being granted permission to go back and rebuild the walls and was also granted the material from the king's forests to do so.

But it was also in chapter two that enemies reared their heads. Chapter two verse ten says:

Nehemiah 2:10 *When Sanballat the Horonite, and Tobiah the servant, the Ammonite, heard of it, it grieved them exceedingly that there was come a man to seek the welfare of the children of Israel.*

It has always grieved the devil and his crowd whenever anyone seeks the welfare of the children of Israel.

When Nehemiah arrived, he did a secret, night-time inspection of the city to see what needed to be done. Then he told the rulers of the city what he had in mind, and they readily agreed to do the job. At that point, a third enemy joined in with Sanballat and Tobiah, a man named Geshem. Undaunted, Nehemiah told them to back off, and that he was going to see the walls rebuilt.

In chapter three we read a detailed account of the people who engaged in the building and of the gates and portions of the wall that they built.

76

In chapter four we found that the people had a mind to work, even if it meant holding a weapon in one hand and a tool in the other. By the time chapter four was done, the wall was joined together all the way around and was at half of its intended height.

In chapter five Nehemiah had to take time to deal with internal problems. These people who had come back out of bondage were enslaving each other. They were charging each other insanely high interest on loans; they were treating each other like the heathens had treated them. Nehemiah led the way in showing everyone how to treat everyone else like they were supposed to.

That brought us to chapter six, when our attention was again brought back to the enemies from without. This time they were much more subtle than before. What they could not accomplish by threats, they tried to accomplish with trickery. Chapter seven is the genealogy of the book.

Nehemiah 7:1 *Now it came to pass, when the wall was built, and I had set up the doors, and the porters and the singers and the Levites were appointed,* **2** *That I gave my brother Hanani, and Hananiah the ruler of the palace, charge over Jerusalem: for he was a faithful man, and feared God above many.* **3** *And I said unto them, Let not the gates of Jerusalem be opened until the sun be hot; and while they stand by, let them shut the doors, and bar them: and appoint watches of the inhabitants of Jerusalem, everyone in his watch, and every one to be over against his house.* **4** *Now the city was large and great: but the people were few therein, and the houses were not builded.*

Nehemiah was preparing to go back to Persia for a time, and he set his brother in charge over the affairs of the city. Hanani has been seen in the book before; he was the man who brought Nehemiah the report of how badly the people and the city were suffering (Nehemiah 1:2).

He told them to keep the gates shut at night, for safety's sake.

Nehemiah 7:5 *And my God put into mine heart to gather together the nobles, and the rulers, and the people, that they might be reckoned by genealogy. And I found a register of the* *genealogy of them which came up at the first, and found written therein,* **6** *These are the children of the province, that went up out of the captivity, of those that had been carried away, whom Nebuchadnezzar the king of Bab7453202487ylon had carried away, and came again to Jerusalem and to Judah, every one unto his city;* **7** *Who came with Zerubbabel, Jeshua, Nehemiah, Azariah, Raamiah, Nahamani, Mordecai, Bilshan, Mispereth, Bigvai, Nehum, Baanah. The number, I say, of the men of the people of Israel was this;* **8** *The children of Parosh, two thousand an hundred seventy and two.* **9** *The children of Shephatiah, three hundred seventy and two.* **10** *The children of Arah, six hundred fifty and two.* **11** *The children of Pahathmoab, of the children of Jeshua and Joab, two thousand and eight hundred and eighteen.* **12** *The children of Elam, a thousand two hundred fifty and four.* **13** *The children of Zattu, eight hundred forty and five.* **14** *The children of Zaccai, seven hundred and threescore.* **15** *The children of Binnui, six hundred forty and eight.* **16** *The children of Bebai, six hundred twenty and eight.* **17** *The children of Azgad, two thousand three hundred twenty and two.* **18** *The children of Adonikam, six hundred threescore and seven.* **19** *The children of Bigvai, two thousand threescore and seven.* **20** *The children of Adin, six hundred fifty and five.* **21** *The children of Ater of Hezekiah, ninety and eight.* **22** *The children of Hashum, three hundred twenty and eight.* **23** *The children of Bezai, three hundred twenty and four.* **24** *The children of Hariph, an hundred and twelve.* **25** *The children of Gibeon, ninety and five.* **26** *The men of Bethlehem and Netophah, an hundred fourscore and eight.* **27** *The men of Anathoth, an hundred twenty and eight.* **28** *The men of Bethazmaveth, forty and two.* **29** *The men of Kirjathjearim, Chephirah, and Beeroth, seven hundred forty and three.* **30** *The men of Ramah and Geba, six hundred twenty and one.* **31** *The men of Michmas, an hundred and twenty and two.* **32** *The men of Bethel and Ai, an hundred twenty and three.* **33** *The men of the other Nebo, fifty and two.* **34** *The children of the other Elam, a thousand two hundred fifty and four.* **35** *The children of Harim, three hundred and twenty.* **36** *The children of Jericho, three hundred forty and five.* **37** *The children of Lod, Hadid, and Ono, seven hundred twenty and one.* **38** *The children of Senaah, three* *thousand nine hundred and thirty.* **39** *The priests: the children of Jedaiah, of the house of Jeshua, nine hundred seventy and three.* **40** *The children of Immer, a thousand fifty and two.* **41** *The children of Pashur, a thousand two hundred forty and seven.* **42** *The children of Harim, a thousand and seventeen.* **43** *The Levites: the children of Jeshua, of Kadmiel, and of the children of Hodevah, seventy and four.* **44** *The singers: the children of Asaph, an hundred forty and eight.* **45** *The porters: the children of Shallum, the children of Ater, the children of Talmon, the children of Akkub, the children of Hatita, the children of Shobai, an hundred thirty and eight.* **46** *The Nethinims: the children of Ziha, the children of Hashupha, the children of Tabbaoth,* **47** *The children of Keros, the children of Sia, the children of Padon,* **48** *The children of Lebana, the children of Hagaba, the children of Shalmai,* **49** *The children of Hanan, the children of Giddel, the children of Gahar,* **50** *The children of Reaiah, the children of Rezin, the children of Nekoda,* **51** *The children of Gazzam, the children of Uzza, the children of Phaseah,* **52** *The children of Besai, the children of Meunim, the children of Nephishesim,* **53** *The children of Bakbuk, the children of Hakupha, the children of Harhur,* **54** *The children of Bazlith, the children of Mehida, the children of Harsha,* **55** *The children of Barkos, the children of Sisera, the children of Tamah,* **56** *The children of Neziah, the children of Hatipha.* **57** *The children of Solomon's servants: the children of Sotai, the children of Sophereth, the children of Perida,* **58** *The children of Jaala, the children of Darkon, the children of Giddel,* **59** *The children of Shephatiah, the children of Hattil, the children of Pochereth of Zebaim, the children of Amon.* **60** *All the Nethinims, and the children of Solomon's servants, were three hundred ninety and two.* **61** *And these were they which went up also from Telmelah, Telharesha, Cherub, Addon, and Immer: but they could not shew their father's house, nor their seed, whether they were of Israel.* **62** *The children of Delaiah, the children of Tobiah, the children of Nekoda, six hundred forty and two.* **63** *And of the priests: the children of Habaiah, the children of Koz, the children of Barzillai, which took one of the daughters of Barzillai the Gileadite to wife, and was called after their name.* **64** *These sought their register among those that were reckoned by genealogy, but it was not* *found: therefore were they, as polluted, put from the priesthood.* **65** *And the Tirshatha said unto them, that they should not eat of the most holy things, till there stood up a priest with Urim and Thummim.* **66** *The whole congregation together was forty and two thousand three hundred and threescore,* **67** *Beside their manservants and their maidservants, of whom there were seven thousand three hundred thirty and seven: and they had two hundred forty and five singing men and singing women.* **68** *Their horses, seven hundred thirty and six: their mules, two hundred forty and five:* **69** *Their camels, four hundred thirty and five: six thousand seven hundred and twenty asses.* **70** *And some of the chief of the fathers gave unto the work. The Tirshatha gave to the treasure a thousand drams of gold, fifty basons, five hundred and thirty priests' garments.* **71** *And some of the chief of the fathers gave to the treasure of the work twenty thousand drams of gold, and two thousand and two hundred pound of silver.* **72** *And that which the rest of the people gave was twenty thousand drams of gold, and two thousand pound of silver, and threescore and seven priests' garments.* **73** *So the priests, and the Levites, and the porters, and the singers, and some of the people, and the Nethinims, and all Israel, dwelt in their cities; and when the seventh month came, the children of Israel were in their cities.*

This genealogical list is nearly identical to the one recorded in Ezra chapter two. It has some slight differences because this one was taken forty years later, and families grow bigger or smaller during the years.

The overarching lesson to be learned from this list, though, is that God wanted them to remember who came before them. It was God who put this into Nehemiah's heart. We do well, even though no one is perfect, to never forget names like Rice, Ray, Norris, Sightler, Greene, Truett, Jones, Spurgeon, Roberson...

Chapter Eight
An Eight Day Revival

Nehemiah 8:1 *And all the people gathered themselves together as one man into the street that was before the water gate; and they spake unto Ezra the scribe to bring the book of the law of Moses, which the LORD had commanded to Israel.* **2** *And Ezra the priest brought the law before the congregation both of men and women, and all that could hear with understanding, upon the first day of the seventh month.* **3** *And he read therein before the street that was before the water gate from the morning until midday, before the men and the women, and those that could understand; and the ears of all the people were attentive unto the book of the law.* **4** *And Ezra the scribe stood upon a pulpit of wood, which they had made for the purpose; and beside him stood Mattithiah, and Shema, and Anaiah, and Urijah, and Hilkiah, and Maaseiah, on his right hand; and on his left hand, Pedaiah, and Mishael, and Malchiah, and Hashum, and Hashbadana, Zechariah, and Meshullam.* **5** *And Ezra opened the book in the sight of all the people; (for he was above all the people;) and when he opened it, all the people stood up:* **6** *And Ezra blessed the LORD, the great God. And all the people answered, Amen, Amen, with lifting up their hands: and they bowed their heads, and worshipped the LORD with their faces to the ground.* **7** *Also Jeshua, and Bani, and Sherebiah, Jamin, Akkub, Shabbethai, Hodijah, Maaseiah, Kelita, Azariah, Jozabad, Hanan, Pelaiah,* *and the Levites, caused the people to understand the law: and the people stood in their place. 8 So they read in the book in the law of God distinctly, and gave the sense, and caused them to understand the reading. 9 And Nehemiah, which is the Tirshatha, and Ezra the priest the scribe, and the Levites that taught the people, said unto all the people, This day is holy unto the LORD your God; mourn not, nor weep. For all the people wept, when they heard the words of the law. 10 Then he said unto them, Go your way, eat the fat, and drink the sweet, and send portions unto them for whom nothing is prepared: for this day is holy unto our Lord: neither be ye sorry; for the joy of the LORD is your strength. 11 So the Levites stilled all the people, saying, Hold your peace, for the day is holy; neither be ye grieved. 12 And all the people went their way to eat, and to drink, and to send portions, and to make great mirth, because they had understood the words that were declared unto them. 13 And on the second day were gathered together the chief of the fathers of all the people, the priests, and the Levites, unto Ezra the scribe, even to understand the words of the law. 14 And they found written in the law which the LORD had commanded by Moses, that the children of Israel should dwell in booths in the feast of the seventh month: 15 And that they should publish and proclaim in all their cities, and in Jerusalem, saying, Go forth unto the mount, and fetch olive branches, and pine branches, and myrtle branches, and palm branches, and branches of thick trees, to make booths, as it is written. 16 So the people went forth, and brought them, and made themselves booths, every one upon the roof of his house, and in their courts, and in the courts of the house of God, and in the street of the water gate, and in the street of the gate of Ephraim. 17 And all the congregation of them that were come again out of the captivity made booths, and sat under the booths: for since the days of Jeshua the son of Nun unto that day had not the children of Israel done so. And there was very great gladness. 18 Also day by day, from the first day unto the last day, he read in the book of the law of God. And they kept the feast seven days; and on the eighth day was a solemn assembly, according unto the manner.*

Chapter seven was a long chapter, seventy-three verses, and in it Nehemiah took a genealogy and census of the people.

And that brings us to chapter eight, which centers around an amazing eight day revival.

The Call for the Preacher

Nehemiah 8:1 *And all the people gathered themselves together as one man into the street that was before the water gate; and they spake unto Ezra the scribe to bring the book of the law of Moses, which the LORD had commanded to Israel.*

Ezra the scribe had been back for thirteen years now. I do not know how much preaching he did during those years, but I do know that now he received an invitation to do a city-wide crusade. People wanted something; they wanted to hear from the Bible. This is what God's real people always want.

Nehemiah 8:2 *And Ezra the priest brought the law before the congregation both of men and women, and all that could hear with understanding, upon the first day of the seventh month.*

Way back then, the preacher was preaching both to men and women. This should make us wonder how some of the brethren through the years have come to the odd conclusion that men and women should not go to church together, but that the women should stay home and let their husbands teach them when they get back.

Nehemiah 8:3 *And he read therein before the street that was before the water gate from the morning until midday, before the men and the women, and those that could understand; and the ears of all the people were attentive unto the book of the law.*

In his message, the entire morning was spent just reading the text of Scripture. Preacher, please do not ever say, "For time's sake I won't read my entire text, just skip ahead to..."

If you actually read much Scripture during your message, it may be that God the Holy Ghost pricks someone's heart with a verse that you are not even focusing on! What God says is more important than what you have to say about what God says!

Nehemiah 8:4 *And Ezra the scribe stood upon a pulpit of wood, which they had made for the purpose; and beside him stood Mattithiah, and Shema, and Anaiah, and Urijah, and Hilkiah, and Maaseiah, on his right hand; and on his left hand,*

Pedaiah, and Mishael, and Malchiah, and Hashum, and Hashbadana, Zechariah, and Meshullam.

This is the only mention of a pulpit in the Bible. It was something to elevate Ezra to where he could be seen and heard.

Nehemiah 8:5 *And Ezra opened the book in the sight of all the people; (for he was above all the people;) and when he opened it, all the people stood up:*

When the text of Scripture was read, all the people stood up. This is a tremendous sign of respect. I do this in my preaching. It is a good visual reminder that the Bible is not like any other book.

Nehemiah 8:6 *And Ezra blessed the LORD, the great God. And all the people answered, Amen, Amen, with lifting up their hands: and they bowed their heads, and worshipped the LORD with their faces to the ground.*

There are some wonderful things to observe in this verse:

People saying amen, amen, during the preaching...

People lifting up their hands...

People bowing their heads and putting their faces to the ground...

Dried up professor-types in the ministry have tried their best to kill this, and in so doing they have sucked the life out of Christianity. No wonder Islam is capturing the fancy of Americans now. They are wrong, but they have the energy and excitement that is lacking from those who are right!

Nehemiah 8:7 *Also Jeshua, and Bani, and Sherebiah, Jamin, Akkub, Shabbethai, Hodijah, Maaseiah, Kelita, Azariah, Jozabad, Hanan, Pelaiah, and the Levites, caused the people to understand the law: and the people stood in their place.*

The law was written in Hebrew, and Ezra read it as such. But many of the people had lost their native tongue and spoke only Chaldee or Syriak. These men translated what he was saying to them and explained it.

Nehemiah 8:8 *So they read in the book in the law of God distinctly, and gave the sense, and caused them to understand the reading.*

Listen very carefully; this verse explains what preaching is supposed to be all about. Read God's Word very clearly, give people the *sense* of it, meaning put it in words they can grasp, then cause them to *understand* it, meaning "to discern," to apply it to their lives. When a preacher is done preaching a message the people who have heard him ought to know what the Bible actually said, what those words actually mean, and how they are supposed to apply it in their own lives.

The new walls would never last if they were not accompanied by revived hearts, and Nehemiah and Ezra knew this!

The Comfort for the People

Nehemiah 8:9 *And Nehemiah, which is the Tirshatha* **(this word means "governor")**, *and Ezra the priest the scribe, and the Levites that taught the people, said unto all the people, This day is holy unto the LORD your God; mourn not, nor weep. For all the people wept, when they heard the words of the law.*

Have you ever read the Law of Moses? It would definitely be enough to make you cry, realize your shortcomings, and the judgements that could fall from them.

Nehemiah 8:10 *Then he said unto them, Go your way, eat the fat, and drink the sweet, and send portions unto them for whom nothing is prepared: for this day is holy unto our Lord: neither be ye sorry; for the joy of the LORD is your strength.* **11** *So the Levites stilled all the people, saying, Hold your peace, for the day is holy; neither be ye grieved.*

There is a time to wail on people and make them feel miserable. There is also a time to bind up their wounds and bring them comfort. Preacher, never let all of your messages be "blood and guts."

Nehemiah 8:12 *And all the people went their way to eat, and to drink, and to send portions, and to make great mirth, because they had understood the words that were declared unto them.*

Both the words of Scripture and the words of comfort caused them to rejoice. We thank you, Lord, for allowing us that blessed privilege!

The Cry from the Past

Nehemiah 8:13 *And on the second day were gathered together the chief of the fathers of all the people, the priests, and* *the Levites, unto Ezra the scribe, even to understand the words of the law.* **14** *And they found written in the law which the LORD had commanded by Moses, that the children of Israel should dwell in booths in the feast of the seventh month:* **15** *And that they should publish and proclaim in all their cities, and in Jerusalem, saying, Go forth unto the mount, and fetch olive branches, and pine branches, and myrtle branches, and palm branches, and branches of thick trees, to make booths, as it is written.*

The verses above are speaking of the Feast of Tabernacles, which was a time of great joy. It made their minds hearken back to the years of the wilderness wanderings, years when, despite their disobedience, God tabernacled with them.

Nehemiah 8:16 *So the people went forth, and brought them, and made themselves booths, every one upon the roof of his house, and in their courts, and in the courts of the house of God, and in the street of the water gate, and in the street of the gate of Ephraim.* **17** *And all the congregation of them that were come again out of the captivity made booths, and sat under the booths: for since the days of Jeshua the son of Nun unto that day had not the children of Israel done so. And there was very great gladness.*

They had just finished building the wall, and then they had to go build booths. Why? Because our relationship with God is more important to build than any earthly, "permanent" structure. These booths, temporary though they may have seemed, were a reminder of the permanent: their relationship with God. The wall of the city, permanent though it may have seemed, was actually temporary and would one day be torn down.

Nehemiah 8:18 *Also day by day, from the first day unto the last day, he read in the book of the law of God. And they kept the feast seven days; and on the eighth day was a solemn assembly, according unto the manner.*

Though a bit wordy, Jamison, Fausset, and Brown give a good explanation of this verse:

> "The feast of tabernacles was brought to
> a close on the eighth day, which was the great day

(Le 23:39). Besides the common routine sacrifices, there were special offerings appointed for that day though these were fewer than on any of the preceding days; and there were also, as was natural on that occasion when vast multitudes were convened for a solemn religious purpose, many spontaneous gifts and services, so that there was full scope for the exercise of a devout spirit in the people, both for their obedience to the statutory offerings, and by the presentation of those which were made by free will or in consequence of vows." JFB

This great day of the feast would one day, a few generations later, become the day on which Jesus offered Himself as water to those who were thirsting. The joy was missed by the hearers on that day, but it was not missed by those in Nehemiah's time. Solemn assembly, yes, but due to their success in building the wall, utterly joyful as well.

Chapter Nine
Stand Up and Bless the Lord

Nehemiah 9:1 *Now in the twenty and fourth day of this month the children of Israel were assembled with fasting, and with sackclothes, and earth upon them. 2 And the seed of Israel separated themselves from all strangers, and stood and confessed their sins, and the iniquities of their fathers. 3 And they stood up in their place, and read in the book of the law of the LORD their God one fourth part of the day; and another fourth part they confessed, and worshipped the LORD their God. 4 Then stood up upon the stairs, of the Levites, Jeshua, and Bani, Kadmiel, Shebaniah, Bunni, Sherebiah, Bani, and Chenani, and cried with a loud voice unto the LORD their God. 5 Then the Levites, Jeshua, and Kadmiel, Bani, Hashabniah, Sherebiah, Hodijah, Shebaniah, and Pethahiah, said, Stand up and bless the LORD your God for ever and ever: and blessed be thy glorious name, which is exalted above all blessing and praise. 6 Thou, even thou, art LORD alone; thou hast made heaven, the heaven of heavens, with all their host, the earth, and all things that are therein, the seas, and all that is therein, and thou preservest them all; and the host of heaven worshippeth thee. 7 Thou art the LORD the God, who didst choose Abram, and broughtest him forth out of Ur of the Chaldees, and gavest him the name of Abraham; 8 And foundest his heart faithful before thee, and madest a covenant with him to give the land of the Canaanites, the Hittites, the Amorites, and the Perizzites, and the Jebusites,* *and the Girgashites, to give it, I say, to his seed, and hast performed thy words; for thou art righteous:* **9** *And didst see the affliction of our fathers in Egypt, and heardest their cry by the Red sea;* **10** *And shewedst signs and wonders upon Pharaoh, and on all his servants, and on all the people of his land: for thou knewest that they dealt proudly against them. So didst thou get thee a name, as it is this day.* **11** *And thou didst divide the sea before them, so that they went through the midst of the sea on the dry land; and their persecutors thou threwest into the deeps, as a stone into the mighty waters.* **12** *Moreover thou leddest them in the day by a cloudy pillar; and in the night by a pillar of fire, to give them light in the way wherein they should go.* **13** *Thou camest down also upon mount Sinai, and spakest with them from heaven, and gavest them right judgments, and true laws, good statutes and commandments:* **14** *And madest known unto them thy holy sabbath, and commandedst them precepts, statutes, and laws, by the hand of Moses thy servant:* **15** *And gavest them bread from heaven for their hunger, and broughtest forth water for them out of the rock for their thirst, and promisedst them that they should go in to possess the land which thou hadst sworn to give them.* **16** *But they and our fathers dealt proudly, and hardened their necks, and hearkened not to thy commandments,* **17** *And refused to obey, neither were mindful of thy wonders that thou didst among them; but hardened their necks, and in their rebellion appointed a captain to return to their bondage: but thou art a God ready to pardon, gracious and merciful, slow to anger, and of great kindness, and forsookest them not.* **18** *Yea, when they had made them a molten calf, and said, This is thy God that brought thee up out of Egypt, and had wrought great provocations;* **19** *Yet thou in thy manifold mercies forsookest them not in the wilderness: the pillar of the cloud departed not from them by day, to lead them in the way; neither the pillar of fire by night, to shew them light, and the way wherein they should go.* **20** *Thou gavest also thy good spirit to instruct them, and withheldest not thy manna from their mouth, and gavest them water for their thirst.* **21** *Yea, forty years didst thou sustain them in the wilderness, so that they lacked nothing; their clothes waxed not old, and their feet swelled not.* **22** *Moreover thou gavest them kingdoms and nations, and didst* divide them into corners: so they possessed the land of Sihon, and the land of the king of Heshbon, and the land of Og king of Bashan. **23** Their children also multipliedst thou as the stars of heaven, and broughtest them into the land, concerning which thou hadst promised to their fathers, that they should go in to possess it. **24** So the children went in and possessed the land, and thou subduedst before them the inhabitants of the land, the Canaanites, and gavest them into their hands, with their kings, and the people of the land, that they might do with them as they would. **25** And they took strong cities, and a fat land, and possessed houses full of all goods, wells digged, vineyards, and oliveyards, and fruit trees in abundance: so they did eat, and were filled, and became fat, and delighted themselves in thy great goodness. **26** Nevertheless they were disobedient, and rebelled against thee, and cast thy law behind their backs, and slew thy prophets which testified against them to turn them to thee, and they wrought great provocations. **27** Therefore thou deliveredst them into the hand of their enemies, who vexed them: and in the time of their trouble, when they cried unto thee, thou heardest them from heaven; and according to thy manifold mercies thou gavest them saviours, who saved them out of the hand of their enemies. **28** But after they had rest, they did evil again before thee: therefore leftest thou them in the hand of their enemies, so that they had the dominion over them: yet when they returned, and cried unto thee, thou heardest them from heaven; and many times didst thou deliver them according to thy mercies; **29** And testifiedst against them, that thou mightest bring them again unto thy law: yet they dealt proudly, and hearkened not unto thy commandments, but sinned against thy judgments, (which if a man do, he shall live in them;) and withdrew the shoulder, and hardened their neck, and would not hear. **30** Yet many years didst thou forbear them, and testifiedst against them by thy spirit in thy prophets: yet would they not give ear: therefore gavest thou them into the hand of the people of the lands. **31** Nevertheless for thy great mercies' sake thou didst not utterly consume them, nor forsake them; for thou art a gracious and merciful God. **32** Now therefore, our God, the great, the mighty, and the terrible God, who keepest covenant and mercy, let not all the trouble seem little before thee, that *hath come upon us, on our kings, on our princes, and on our priests, and on our prophets, and on our fathers, and on all thy people, since the time of the kings of Assyria unto this day.* **33** *Howbeit thou art just in all that is brought upon us; for thou hast done right, but we have done wickedly:* **34** *Neither have our kings, our princes, our priests, nor our fathers, kept thy law, nor hearkened unto thy commandments and thy testimonies, wherewith thou didst testify against them.* **35** *For they have not served thee in their kingdom, and in thy great goodness that thou gavest them, and in the large and fat land which thou gavest before them, neither turned they from their wicked works.* **36** *Behold, we are servants this day, and for the land that thou gavest unto our fathers to eat the fruit thereof and the good thereof, behold, we are servants in it:* **37** *And it yieldeth much increase unto the kings whom thou hast set over us because of our sins: also they have dominion over our bodies, and over our cattle, at their pleasure, and we are in great distress.* **38** *And because of all this we make a sure covenant, and write it; and our princes, Levites, and priests, seal unto it.*

Chapter eight dealt with the eight day revival. The people came to a city-wide preaching meeting and found that they were supposed to be keeping the Feast of Tabernacles. A day of weeping turned into the happiest of holidays. God's timing was perfect, and He knew His hard working people needed to rejoice for a while. And that brings us to chapter nine, where we will find the people standing to bless the Lord.

I do not want to get too far ahead, but let me give you a great quote from Adam Clarke, commenting on a verse we will read in just a moment:

"It is the shameless custom of many congregations of people to sit still while they profess to bless and praise God, by singing the Psalms of David or hymns made on the plan of the Gospel! I ask such persons, Did they ever feel the spirit of devotion while thus employed? If they do, it must be owned that, by the prevalence of habit, they have counteracted the influence of an attitude most friendly to such acts of devotion."

Awesome quote! In other words, how can you actually say that you are blessing and praising God while sitting on your posterior and not moving anything but your lips?

A Time of Sorrowing
Nehemiah 9:1 *Now in the twenty and fourth day of this month the children of Israel were assembled with fasting, and with sackclothes, and earth upon them.*

In chapter eight the people had heard the words of the law read, and they wept. Nehemiah and the priests told them not to weep. God saw what they had just been through. A time of rejoicing followed, the seven days of the Feast of Tabernacles, followed by the eighth day, often called the great day of the feast. Chapter nine begins on the very next day. After rejoicing, after enjoying their relationship with the God of Israel, the people were then ready to actually deal with their sin. That sounds like the exact opposite of how we always expect things to be! Normally, God requires that we deal with our sin, and then the rejoicing follows. But on this occasion, it was not a willful sin being dealt with. The people simply did not know the part of God's law that they had been neglecting. So in mercy, God told them to rejoice, and then the sin was dealt with.

We are not God, and God is very merciful!

A Time of Separating
Nehemiah 9:2 *And the seed of Israel separated themselves from all strangers, and stood and confessed their sins, and the iniquities of their fathers. 3 And they stood up in their place, and read in the book of the law of the LORD their God one fourth part of the day; and another fourth part they confessed, and worshipped the LORD their God.*

Strangers were spoken of in this verse. These were not just foreigners, those could and often did become proselytes to the Jewish religion. The word indicates those who wanted to reject God yet still intermingle with God's people. God has always been opposed to that arrangement:

93

Amos 3:3 *Can two walk together, except they be agreed?*

Psalm 1:1 *Blessed is the man that walketh not in the counsel of the ungodly, nor standeth in the way of sinners, nor sitteth in the seat of the scornful.* **2** *But his delight is in the law of the LORD; and in his law doth he meditate day and night.* **3** *And he shall be like a tree planted by the rivers of water, that bringeth forth his fruit in his season; his leaf also shall not wither; and whatsoever he doeth shall prosper.*

2 Corinthians 6:17 *Wherefore come out from among them, and be ye separate, saith the Lord, and touch not the unclean thing; and I will receive you,* **18** *And will be a Father unto you, and ye shall be my sons and daughters, saith the Lord Almighty.*

They separated from those who would hinder their walk with God. They also spent time confessing their own sin. Any "revival" that just makes you despise the wicked without ever examining the wickedness of your own heart has not been a real revival; it has been a political convention.

A Time of Shouting

Nehemiah 9:4 *Then stood up upon the stairs, of the Levites, Jeshua, and Bani, Kadmiel, Shebaniah, Bunni, Sherebiah, Bani, and Chenani, and cried with a loud voice unto the LORD their God.*

Here are more people who apparently did not know that crying out with a loud voice unto God is "indecent and out of order." Oh, how I wish those poor deluded souls could have taken a few classes at the average Bible college...

Nehemiah 9:5 *Then the Levites, Jeshua, and Kadmiel, Bani, Hashabniah, Sherebiah, Hodijah, Shebaniah, and Pethahiah, said, Stand up and bless the LORD your God for ever and ever: and blessed be thy glorious name, which is exalted above all blessing and praise.*

This is the verse I took that quote from by Adam Clarke. Here it is again:

> "It is the shameless custom of many congregations of people to sit still while they profess to bless and praise God, by singing the

Psalms of David or hymns made on the plan of the Gospel! I ask such persons, Did they ever feel the spirit of devotion while thus employed? If they do, it must be owned that, by the prevalence of habit, they have counteracted the influence of an attitude most friendly to such acts of devotion."

Can you imagine this? These carnal, emotional Levites, instructing the people to stand up and bless the Lord? Why, someone should have turned off their microphones, made them leave the platform at once, and then calmed everybody down!

But I wonder, I just wonder, did these guys just maybe actually have something to shout about? Is there a slim possibility that maybe they were actually justified in their "emotional outburst?" Well, let's look through the rest of the chapter and decide on that. You see, in the rest of the chapter, these men gave the reasons why they were shouting and instructing others to do the same.

Nehemiah 9:6 *Thou, even thou, art LORD alone;* **(You are the only One, there is none like You.)** *thou hast made heaven, the heaven of heavens, with all their host, the earth, and all things that are therein, the seas, and all that is therein,* **(You made everything. What a task! But it was easy for You, and You did it in only seven days!)** *and thou preservest them all;* **(You are the glue that holds everything together.)** *and the host of heaven worshippeth thee.* **(Angels worship You, I suppose we should too! Unless, of course, they are being "indecent and out of order.")** 7 *Thou art the LORD the God, who didst choose Abram, and broughtest him forth out of Ur of the Chaldees, and gavest him the name of Abraham;* 8 *And foundest his heart faithful before thee, and madest a covenant with him to give the land of the Canaanites, the Hittites, the Amorites, and the Perizzites, and the Jebusites, and the Girgashites, to give it, I say, to his seed, and hast performed thy words; for thou art righteous:* **(You did the impossible. You chose an old man, waited until he was way past child bearing years, then made him the father of a great nation.)** 9 *And didst see the affliction of our fathers in Egypt, and heardest their* *cry by the Red sea;* **10** *And shewedst signs and wonders upon Pharaoh, and on all his servants, and on all the people of his land: for thou knewest that they dealt proudly against them. So didst thou get thee a name, as it is this day.* **11** *And thou didst divide the sea before them, so that they went through the midst of the sea on the dry land; and their persecutors thou threwest into the deeps, as a stone into the mighty waters.* **12** *Moreover thou leddest them in the day by a cloudy pillar; and in the night by a pillar of fire, to give them light in the way wherein they should go.* **(When Your people were hurting and in anguish, You heard their cry. When they were trapped by the Red Sea, You showed up and made a way.)** **13** *Thou camest down also upon mount Sinai, and spakest with them from heaven, and gavest them right judgments, and true laws, good statutes and commandments:* **(While the rest of the world was mired in superstition, You gave us Your perfect Word!)** **14** *And madest known unto them thy holy Sabbath,* **(You gave them rest.)** *and commandedst them precepts, statutes, and laws, by the hand of Moses thy servant:* **15** *And gavest them bread from heaven for their hunger,* **(When they got hungry, You took the food for the angels of heaven and gave it to men on earth.)** *and broughtest forth water for them out of the rock for their thirst,* **(Water from a rock. Isn't that worth a little "Whoop, Glory!"?)** *and promisedst them that they should go in to possess the land which thou hadst sworn to give them.* **16** *But they and our fathers dealt proudly, and hardened their necks, and hearkened not to thy commandments,* **17** *And refused to obey, neither were mindful of thy wonders that thou didst among them; but hardened their necks, and in their rebellion appointed a captain to return to their bondage: but thou art a God ready to pardon, gracious and merciful, slow to anger, and of great kindness, and forsookest them not.* **(When we deserved to be dropped straight into Hell, You showed up with mercy, grace, and pardon.)** **18** *Yea, when they had made them a molten calf, and said, This is thy God that brought thee up out of Egypt, and had wrought great provocations;* **19** *Yet thou in thy manifold mercies forsookest them not in the wilderness: the pillar of the cloud departed not from them by day, to lead them in the way; neither the pillar of fire by night, to shew them light, and the way* *wherein they should go.* **(When we rejected You, You didn't reject us.) 20** *Thou gavest also thy good spirit to instruct them, and withheldest not thy manna from their mouth, and gavest them water for their thirst.* **21** *Yea, forty years didst thou sustain them in the wilderness, so that they lacked nothing; their clothes waxed not old, and their feet swelled not.* **(When You should have left us to fend for ourselves and make our own way, scratching through garbage cans for food, You kept on providing for our needs anyway.) 22** *Moreover thou gavest them kingdoms and nations, and didst divide them into corners: so they possessed the land of Sihon, and the land of the king of Heshbon, and the land of Og king of Bashan.* **(We treated You like an enemy, but You treated us like a friend. You went out and defeated our enemies for us when You should have let them overrun us.) 23** *Their children also multipliedst thou as the stars of heaven, and broughtest them into the land, concerning which thou hadst promised to their fathers, that they should go in to possess it.* **(You gave us lots of kids!) 24** *So the children went in and possessed the land, and thou subduedst before them the inhabitants of the land, the Canaanites, and gavest them into their hands, with their kings, and the people of the land, that they might do with them as they would.* **25** *And they took strong cities, and a fat land, and possessed houses full of all goods, wells digged, vineyards, and oliveyards, and fruit trees in abundance: so they did eat, and were filled, and became fat, and delighted themselves in thy great goodness.* **(You gave us fully matured blessings, instead of making us "work our way up the corporate ladder.") 26** *Nevertheless they were disobedient, and rebelled against thee, and cast thy law behind their backs, and slew thy prophets which testified against them to turn them to thee, and they wrought great provocations.* **27** *Therefore thou deliveredst them into the hand of their enemies, who vexed them: and in the time of their trouble, when they cried unto thee, thou heardest them from heaven; and according to thy manifold mercies thou gavest them saviours, who saved them out of the hand of their enemies.* **(After all the good things You did for us, we rebelled against You. You punished us, and You had every right to do so. But then, amazingly, when we started to cry and be sorry for our sins, You forgave us. We**

wouldn't have done that for others, but You did it for us!) 28 *But after they had rest, they did evil again before thee: therefore leftest thou them in the hand of their enemies, so that they had the dominion over them: yet when they returned, and cried unto thee, thou heardest them from heaven; and many times didst thou deliver them according to thy mercies;* **(Sound familiar? What a pattern. Do You ever get tired of us, God? Thank God, I'm so glad that You don't!) 29** *And testifiedst against them, that thou mightest bring them again unto thy law: yet they dealt proudly, and hearkened not unto thy commandments, but sinned against thy judgments, (which if a man do, he shall live in them;) and withdrew the shoulder, and hardened their neck, and would not hear.* **30** *Yet many years didst thou forbear them, and testifiedst against them by thy spirit in thy prophets: yet would they not give ear: therefore gavest thou them into the hand of the people of the lands.* **31** *Nevertheless for thy great mercies' sake thou didst not utterly consume them, nor forsake them; for thou art a gracious and merciful God.* **(That brings us to the modern day. Here we are, God, at the tail end of that same pattern. Thank You, God, for not giving up on us!)**

That is quite a lot to shout about! But notice this: people who shout are accused of being "shallow, emotional, weak-minded." But look at the deep and spiritual conclusions that their shouting led them to:

32 *Now therefore, our God, the great, the mighty, and the terrible God, who keepest covenant and mercy, let not all the trouble seem little before thee, that hath come upon us, on our kings, on our princes, and on our priests, and on our prophets, and on our fathers, and on all thy people, since the time of the kings of Assyria unto this day.* **33** *Howbeit thou art just in all that is brought upon us; for thou hast done right, but we have done wickedly:* **("God, we deserve the whippings we have received." See the humility, as opposed to the pride of the "Non-emotional crowd.")** **34** *Neither have our kings, our princes, our priests, nor our fathers, kept thy law, nor hearkened unto thy commandments and thy testimonies, wherewith thou didst testify against them.* **35** *For they have not served thee in their kingdom, and in thy great goodness that thou gavest them, and in the large and fat land which thou gavest before them,* *neither turned they from their wicked works.* **(God, we did not sin because we were "deprived," we sinned because we wanted to. We sinned in spite of our great blessings!) 36** *Behold, we are servants this day, and for the land that thou gavest unto our fathers to eat the fruit thereof and the good thereof, behold, we are servants in it: 37 And it yieldeth much increase unto the kings whom thou hast set over us because of our sins: also they have dominion over our bodies, and over our cattle, at their pleasure, and we are in great distress.* **(God, we are right now, this moment, seeing our blessings go to others. And it is all because of the law of sowing and reaping.) 38** *And because of all this we make a sure covenant, and write it; and our princes, Levites, and priests, seal unto it.* **(God, we are putting it in writing that we are going to serve You. We are not going to be like people that say, "Well, I am not going to make any promises..." No, we are making a promise. We are promising in writing that we are going to serve You...)**

That is some good, deep, solid, Scriptural reasoning from people who were so "emotional and shallow" that they stood and shouted, praising God, and instructed others to do so also.

Chapter Ten
Sealing the Deal

Nehemiah 10:1 *Now those that sealed were, Nehemiah, the Tirshatha, the son of Hachaliah, and Zidkijah,* **2** *Seraiah, Azariah, Jeremiah,* **3** *Pashur, Amariah, Malchijah,* **4** *Hattush, Shebaniah, Malluch,* **5** *Harim, Meremoth, Obadiah,* **6** *Daniel, Ginnethon, Baruch,* **7** *Meshullam, Abijah, Mijamin,* **8** *Maaziah, Bilgai, Shemaiah: these were the priests.* **9** *And the Levites: both Jeshua the son of Azaniah, Binnui of the sons of Henadad, Kadmiel;* **10** *And their brethren, Shebaniah, Hodijah, Kelita, Pelaiah, Hanan,* **11** *Micha, Rehob, Hashabiah,* **12** *Zaccur, Sherebiah, Shebaniah,* **13** *Hodijah, Bani, Beninu.* **14** *The chief of the people; Parosh, Pahathmoab, Elam, Zatthu, Bani,* **15** *Bunni, Azgad, Bebai,* **16** *Adonijah, Bigvai, Adin,* **17** *Ater, Hizkijah, Azzur,* **18** *Hodijah, Hashum, Bezai,* **19** *Hariph, Anathoth, Nebai,* **20** *Magpiash, Meshullam, Hezir,* **21** *Meshezabeel, Zadok, Jaddua,* **22** *Pelatiah, Hanan, Anaiah,* **23** *Hoshea, Hananiah, Hashub,* **24** *Hallohesh, Pileha, Shobek,* **25** *Rehum, Hashabnah, Maaseiah,* **26** *And Ahijah, Hanan, Anan,* **27** *Malluch, Harim, Baanah.* **28** *And the rest of the people, the priests, the Levites, the porters, the singers, the Nethinims, and all they that had separated themselves from the people of the lands unto the law of God, their wives, their sons, and their daughters, every one having knowledge, and having understanding;* **29** *They clave to their brethren, their nobles, and entered into a curse, and into an oath, to walk in God's law,* *which was given by Moses the servant of God, and to observe and do all the commandments of the LORD our Lord, and his judgments and his statutes;* **30** *And that we would not give our daughters unto the people of the land, nor take their daughters for our sons:* **31** *And if the people of the land bring ware or any victuals on the sabbath day to sell, that we would not buy it of them on the sabbath, or on the holy day: and that we would leave the seventh year, and the exaction of every debt.* **32** *Also we made ordinances for us, to charge ourselves yearly with the third part of a shekel for the service of the house of our God;* **33** *For the shewbread, and for the continual meat offering, and for the continual burnt offering, of the sabbaths, of the new moons, for the set feasts, and for the holy things, and for the sin offerings to make an atonement for Israel, and for all the work of the house of our God.* **34** *And we cast the lots among the priests, the Levites, and the people, for the wood offering, to bring it into the house of our God, after the houses of our fathers, at times appointed year by year, to burn upon the altar of the LORD our God, as it is written in the law:* **35** *And to bring the firstfruits of our ground, and the firstfruits of all fruit of all trees, year by year, unto the house of the LORD:* **36** *Also the firstborn of our sons, and of our cattle, as it is written in the law, and the firstlings of our herds and of our flocks, to bring to the house of our God, unto the priests that minister in the house of our God:* **37** *And that we should bring the firstfruits of our dough, and our offerings, and the fruit of all manner of trees, of wine and of oil, unto the priests, to the chambers of the house of our God; and the tithes of our ground unto the Levites, that the same Levites might have the tithes in all the cities of our tillage.* **38** *And the priest the son of Aaron shall be with the Levites, when the Levites take tithes: and the Levites shall bring up the tithe of the tithes unto the house of our God, to the chambers, into the treasure house.* **39** *For the children of Israel and the children of Levi shall bring the offering of the corn, of the new wine, and the oil, unto the chambers, where are the vessels of the sanctuary, and the priests that minister, and the porters, and the singers: and we will not forsake the house of our God.*

At the end of chapter nine, the very last verse, we read this:

Nehemiah 9:38 *And because of all this we make a sure covenant, and write it; and our princes, Levites, and priests, seal unto it.*

They made decisions on how they would behave, they put it in covenant, contract form, they wrote it out, and they signed their names to it. Chapter ten will give the details of who signed it, and what was in it.

The Primary Signatories

Nehemiah 10:1 *Now those that sealed were, Nehemiah, the Tirshatha, the son of Hachaliah, and Zidkijah, 2 Seraiah, Azariah, Jeremiah, 3 Pashur, Amariah, Malchijah, 4 Hattush, Shebaniah, Malluch, 5 Harim, Meremoth, Obadiah, 6 Daniel, Ginnethon, Baruch, 7 Meshullam, Abijah, Mijamin, 8 Maaziah, Bilgai, Shemaiah: these were the priests. 9 And the Levites: both Jeshua the son of Azaniah, Binnui of the sons of Henadad, Kadmiel; 10 And their brethren, Shebaniah, Hodijah, Kelita, Pelaiah, Hanan, 11 Micha, Rehob, Hashabiah, 12 Zaccur, Sherebiah, Shebaniah, 13 Hodijah, Bani, Beninu. 14 The chief of the people; Parosh, Pahathmoab, Elam, Zatthu, Bani, 15 Bunni, Azgad, Bebai, 16 Adonijah, Bigvai, Adin, 17 Ater, Hizkijah, Azzur, 18 Hodijah, Hashum, Bezai, 19 Hariph, Anathoth, Nebai, 20 Magpiash, Meshullam, Hezir, 21 Meshezabeel, Zadok, Jaddua, 22 Pelatiah, Hanan, Anaiah, 23 Hoshea, Hananiah, Hashub, 24 Hallohesh, Pileha, Shobek, 25 Rehum, Hashabnah, Maaseiah, 26 And Ahijah, Hanan, Anan, 27 Malluch, Harim, Baanah.*

This list gives us four classes of people who signed this document. We first of all find Nehemiah the governor, the one who was in charge. We then find down through the end of verse eight the priests listed. After them we find the Levites in verses nine through thirteen, and then we find the chiefs of the people in verses fourteen through twenty-seven.

Why did only those men sign? For the same reason that only fifty-five men signed the Declaration of Independence. There is only so much room on a document. It is impossible to have everyone sign, so you get representatives to sign it, and those people are basically signing for all of the people.

The Principle Substance

We have seen who signed and that all the people were represented in that signing. So what did they sign their names to? First of all, they signed their names to an agreement to separate *from* the world *to* the law of God

Nehemiah 10:28 *And the rest of the people, the priests, the Levites, the porters, the singers, the Nethinims, and all they that had separated themselves from the people of the lands unto the law of God, their wives, their sons, and their daughters, every one having knowledge, and having understanding;* **29** *They clave to their brethren, their nobles, and entered into a curse, and into an oath, to walk in God's law, which was given by Moses the servant of God, and to observe and do all the commandments of the LORD our Lord, and his judgments and his statutes;*

These verses show what we have just been observing, that in having the nobles sign, they were signing for everyone. Verse twenty-eight wraps all of the rest of the people together into one, whoever was willing to obey, and verse twenty-nine says that they clave to their brethren, their nobles, the ones who had put their names to paper.

These two verses give us the first part of the covenant. It says that they separated themselves from the world to the law of God. Separation is never a negative thing, nor is it ever a positive thing. It is always both a positive and negative thing at the same time. It is impossible to separate yourself from anything without also separating yourself to something else. In other words, every time I draw away from one thing, I am automatically drawing nearer to something else.

This is what is often wrong with our practice of separation. We are always told what to separate *from*, but rarely told what to separate *to*. In that vacuum, people will usually make mistakes. They are told to separate from dressing certain ways, and that is all. But since the other side is not presented, what are they to be separating to, they end up separating from dressing improperly to being proud of how they are no longer dressing, and become arrogant toward others with lower standards.

104

Real separation should tell us what to separate *from* and then direct us *to* separate to everything about Christ and His Word. Real separation like that will not just make us outwardly acceptable but will also produce in us a right attitude, a right spirit, a right demeanor.

Now please understand this. If we are ever going to separate from the world, we must replace what we have separated from with a separation to the Word of God. Many people separate from the world to the opinions of a pastor. Many people separate from the world to the customs of a church or cult. Men of God must be in the habit of teaching people to separate from the world, to the Word.

The second thing they signed their names to was an agreement never to allow their children to intermarry with non-believers:

Nehemiah 10:30 *And that we would not give our daughters unto the people of the land, nor take their daughters for our sons:*

In those days parents took an authoritative role in who their children married. They literally arranged the marriages. I am not necessarily in favor of arranged marriages, but I do believe that they were closer to right than we usually are in this day where the children arrange the marriages and the parents' only role is to pay for it. Parents, your say should mean more than anyone else's in who the children marry. You know your children better than they know themselves! Parents, you should never, ever, under any circumstances, put your blessings on your children marrying unbelievers. God's Word is unmistakably clear on this:

2 Corinthians 6:14 *Be ye not unequally yoked together with unbelievers: for what fellowship hath righteousness with unrighteousness? and what communion hath light with darkness?*

There is not an ambiguous word in that text. When it comes to believers marrying unbelievers, the answer is always "No!" God said no about this just as firmly as He said no about homosexuality. Yet many claiming the name of Christ disobey Him on this matter, and then use the Bible as a battering ram when their own children later decide to become Sodomites and

105

lesbians. Sir, Ma'am, if you did not believe the Bible on the one, you will have no credibility telling your children to obey it on the other.

The third part of the agreement was an agreement to operate their personal finances on God's terms, not theirs.

Nehemiah 10:31 *And if the people of the land bring ware or any victuals on the sabbath day to sell, that we would not buy it of them on the sabbath, or on the holy day: and that we would leave the seventh year, and the exaction of every debt.*

The Sabbath was a special part of the covenant, given only to Jews, not Gentiles:

Exodus 31:16 *Wherefore the children of Israel shall keep the sabbath, to observe the sabbath throughout their generations, for a perpetual covenant.* **17** *It is a sign between me and the children of Israel for ever: for in six days the LORD made heaven and earth, and on the seventh day he rested, and was refreshed.*

There were some specific rules they had on the Sabbath, one of which was that they would do no work. In this, the Jews of Nehemiah's day took it even a step farther. They refused to buy from anyone on the Sabbath day, so that others would not work. They wanted that day to be a day of worship, not profit. They decided that on any holy day, they would do this. It was not specifically commanded, but they believed it was what God wanted from them.

Part of their financial promise was that they would obey the command not to sow their fields on the seventh year. That one was actually a specific, written command, not just something they felt like God wanted from them:

Exodus 23:10 *And six years thou shalt sow thy land, and shalt gather in the fruits thereof:* **11** *But the seventh year thou shalt let it rest and lie still; that the poor of thy people may eat: and what they leave the beasts of the field shall eat. In like manner thou shalt deal with thy vineyard, and with thy oliveyard.*

That was a great step of faith. But every time they tried it, it worked! God made the sixth year produce so much that they did not need the seventh. But so often when they saw the great yield on the sixth year, they reasoned, "We can't afford *not* to sow on the seventh!" In fact, it was that very sin that landed them in a seventy-year captivity in Babylon. They disobeyed the command for 490 years; they built up a seventy-year total of Sabbath years that the land did not receive, so God sent them away for seventy years to give the land its rest.

Now they were back from that captivity and anxious to obey!

By the way, a word here might be good. I never beat on anyone who takes the principles of the first part of verse thirty-one and decides for themselves that they will not buy anything on Sunday, they will not go out to eat on Sunday, etc. But I also do not let them beat on me for not having that conviction. For starters, Sunday is not the Sabbath. Secondly, the Sabbath was given to Jews, not Gentiles. But thirdly, and in my mind most importantly, I find it highly inconsistent to observe the pattern of the first part of verse thirty-one and then ignore the pattern of the last half of the very same verse!

If you are going to use the first part of verse thirty-one to prove that we New Testament Christians should not buy or sell on Sunday, then pray tell me why you do not also follow the pattern of the last half of verse thirty-one and refuse to work every seventh year?

But it goes even farther. Verse thirty-one also shows another part of their financial covenant. They agreed to obey Deuteronomy 15:1-2 and forgive every debt on the seventh year:

Deuteronomy 15:1 *At the end of every seven years thou shalt make a release.* **2** *And this is the manner of the release: Every creditor that lendeth ought unto his neighbour shall release it; he shall not exact it of his neighbour, or of his brother; because it is called the LORD'S release.*

I do not ever recall any modern day Christians observing either of those last two practices! What these verses do clearly teach us, though, is to operate our finances on God's terms, not our own. There are hundreds of verses in the Bible on finances that are not specific to the Jews but are for all men everywhere.

The fourth part of their agreement was an agreement to give to maintain the house of God and the work of the ministry:

Nehemiah 10:32 *Also we made ordinances for us, to charge ourselves yearly with the third part of a shekel for the* *service of the house of our God;* **33** *For the shewbread, and for the continual meat offering, and for the continual burnt offering, of the sabbaths, of the new moons, for the set feasts, and for the holy things, and for the sin offerings to make an atonement for Israel, and for all the work of the house of our God.*

This went specifically to the upkeep of and work in the house of God. I know people today are very concerned that they "give to the poor and needy," but the first part of our giving is always to be for the house of God. If people never hear the gospel and get born again, all of the wells and meals and glasses and shoes in the world will not help them.

Nehemiah 10:34 *And we cast the lots among the priests, the Levites, and the people, for the wood offering, to bring it into the house of our God, after the houses of our fathers, at times appointed year by year, to burn upon the altar of the LORD our God, as it is written in the law:* **35** *And to bring the firstfruits of our ground, and the firstfruits of all fruit of all trees, year by year, unto the house of the LORD:* **36** *Also the firstborn of our sons, and of our cattle, as it is written in the law, and the firstlings of our herds and of our flocks, to bring to the house of our God, unto the priests that minister in the house of our God:* **37** *And that we should bring the firstfruits of our dough, and our offerings, and the fruit of all manner of trees, of wine and of oil, unto the priests, to the chambers of the house of our God; and the tithes of our ground unto the Levites, that the same Levites might have the tithes in all the cities of our tillage.*

Verse thirty-four describes what we would call a "special offering" in our day. The law required wood to be brought to the house of God so sacrifices could be made. But all through their history, the Jews had people like the Gibeonites to supply them with that wood. Now there were no more of those around, so they had to draw lots and have a "special offering" to gather the wood. Today it may be for a bus or an update to the bathrooms, but the principle is the same.

Verses thirty-five through thirty-seven describe the tithes off of the things that were not monetary. When they received a gain of any kind, they tithed off of it. They figured out how much it was worth, and they gave the tenth accordingly. That is biblical even for us; it is stated outside of the law:

Proverbs 3:9 *Honour the LORD with thy substance, and with the firstfruits of all thine increase:* **10** *So shall thy barns be filled with plenty, and thy presses shall burst out with new wine.*

You may not always be able to figure it out exactly, but it is a good pattern to follow. For my wife and I, for years we have simplified it by just giving higher than the ten percent required, just to make sure we cover all of the unseen increase. I figure if I am going to make a mistake, I want to make a mistake in giving too much, never in giving too little!

Nehemiah 10:38 *And the priest the son of Aaron shall be with the Levites, when the Levites take tithes: and the Levites shall bring up the tithe of the tithes unto the house of our God, to the chambers, into the treasure house.*

The *tithe of the tithes* was the part that paid the salaries of the men of God (Num. 18:26). Part of their agreement to take care of the house of God and the work of God was to take care of the man of God. I have yet to see God empower and openly approve of a church that did not do this.

Nehemiah 10:39 *For the children of Israel and the children of Levi shall bring the offering of the corn, of the new wine, and the oil, unto the chambers, where are the vessels of the sanctuary, and the priests that minister, and the porters, and the singers:*

The tithe was brought to the place where the preachers and singers and workers were. Today we call that "the church." Tithe does not belong anywhere else.

The fifth part of the agreement was an agreement to actually show up to God's house and be faithful to it:

Nehemiah 10:39b*... and we will not forsake the house of our God.*

These things are right, and we should all be willing to "seal the same deal!"

Chapter Eleven
The Business that Follows the Building

Nehemiah 11:1 *And the rulers of the people dwelt at Jerusalem: the rest of the people also cast lots, to bring one of ten to dwell in Jerusalem the holy city, and nine parts to dwell in other cities. 2 And the people blessed all the men, that willingly offered themselves to dwell at Jerusalem. 3 Now these are the chief of the province that dwelt in Jerusalem: but in the cities of Judah dwelt every one in his possession in their cities, to wit, Israel, the priests, and the Levites, and the Nethinims, and the children of Solomon's servants. 4 And at Jerusalem dwelt certain of the children of Judah, and of the children of Benjamin. Of the children of Judah; Athaiah the son of Uzziah, the son of Zechariah, the son of Amariah, the son of Shephatiah, the son of Mahalaleel, of the children of Perez; 5 And Maaseiah the son of Baruch, the son of Colhozeh, the son of Hazaiah, the son of Adaiah, the son of Joiarib, the son of Zechariah, the son of Shiloni. 6 All the sons of Perez that dwelt at Jerusalem were four hundred threescore and eight valiant men. 7 And these are the sons of Benjamin; Sallu the son of Meshullam, the son of Joed, the son of Pedaiah, the son of Kolaiah, the son of Maaseiah, the son of Ithiel, the son of Jesaiah. 8 And after him Gabbai, Sallai, nine hundred twenty and eight. 9 And Joel the son of Zichri was their overseer: and Judah the son of Senuah was second over the city.* **10** *Of the priests: Jedaiah the son of Joiarib, Jachin.* **11** *Seraiah the son of Hilkiah, the son of Meshullam, the son of Zadok, the son of Meraioth, the son of Ahitub, was the ruler of the house of God.* **12** *And their brethren that did the work of the house were eight hundred twenty and two: and Adaiah the son of Jeroham, the son of Pelaliah, the son of Amzi, the son of Zechariah, the son of Pashur, the son of Malchiah,* **13** *And his brethren, chief of the fathers, two hundred forty and two: and Amashai the son of Azareel, the son of Ahasai, the son of Meshillemoth, the son of Immer,* **14** *And their brethren, mighty men of valour, an hundred twenty and eight: and their overseer was Zabdiel, the son of one of the great men.* **15** *Also of the Levites: Shemaiah the son of Hashub, the son of Azrikam, the son of Hashabiah, the son of Bunni;* **16** *And Shabbethai and Jozabad, of the chief of the Levites, had the oversight of the outward business of the house of God.* **17** *And Mattaniah the son of Micha, the son of Zabdi, the son of Asaph, was the principal to begin the thanksgiving in prayer: and Bakbukiah the second among his brethren, and Abda the son of Shammua, the son of Galal, the son of Jeduthun.* **18** *All the Levites in the holy city were two hundred fourscore and four.* **19** *Moreover the porters, Akkub, Talmon, and their brethren that kept the gates, were an hundred seventy and two.* **20** *And the residue of Israel, of the priests, and the Levites, were in all the cities of Judah, every one in his inheritance.* **21** *But the Nethinims dwelt in Ophel: and Ziha and Gispa were over the Nethinims.* **22** *The overseer also of the Levites at Jerusalem was Uzzi the son of Bani, the son of Hashabiah, the son of Mattaniah, the son of Micha. Of the sons of Asaph, the singers were over the business of the house of God.* **23** *For it was the king's commandment concerning them, that a certain portion should be for the singers, due for every day.* **24** *And Pethahiah the son of Meshezabeel, of the children of Zerah the son of Judah, was at the king's hand in all matters concerning the people.* **25** *And for the villages, with their fields, some of the children of Judah dwelt at Kirjatharba, and in the villages thereof, and at Dibon, and in the villages thereof, and at Jekabzeel, and in the villages thereof,* **26** *And at Jeshua, and at Moladah, and at Bethphelet,* **27** *And at Hazarshual, and at Beersheba, and in the villages thereof,* **28** *And at Ziklag, and at*

Mekonah, and in the villages thereof, **29** And at Enrimmon, and at Zareah, and at Jarmuth, **30** Zanoah, Adullam, and in their villages, at Lachish, and the fields thereof, at Azekah, and in the villages thereof. And they dwelt from Beersheba unto the valley of Hinnom. **31** The children also of Benjamin from Geba dwelt at Michmash, and Aija, and Bethel, and in their villages, **32** And at Anathoth, Nob, Ananiah, **33** Hazor, Ramah, Gittaim, **34** Hadid, Zeboim, Neballat, **35** Lod, and Ono, the valley of craftsmen. **36** And of the Levites were divisions in Judah, and in Benjamin.

    Nehemiah 12:1 Now these are the priests and the Levites that went up with Zerubbabel the son of Shealtiel, and Jeshua: Seraiah, Jeremiah, Ezra, **2** Amariah, Malluch, Hattush, **3** Shechaniah, Rehum, Meremoth, **4** Iddo, Ginnetho, Abijah, **5** Miamin, Maadiah, Bilgah, **6** Shemaiah, and Joiarib, Jedaiah, **7** Sallu, Amok, Hilkiah, Jedaiah. These were the chief of the priests and of their brethren in the days of Jeshua. **8** Moreover the Levites: Jeshua, Binnui, Kadmiel, Sherebiah, Judah, and Mattaniah, which was over the thanksgiving, he and his brethren. **9** Also Bakbukiah and Unni, their brethren, were over against them in the watches. **10** And Jeshua begat Joiakim, Joiakim also begat Eliashib, and Eliashib begat Joiada, **11** And Joiada begat Jonathan, and Jonathan begat Jaddua. **12** And in the days of Joiakim were priests, the chief of the fathers: of Seraiah, Meraiah; of Jeremiah, Hananiah; **13** Of Ezra, Meshullam; of Amariah, Jehohanan; **14** Of Melicu, Jonathan; of Shebaniah, Joseph; **15** Of Harim, Adna; of Meraioth, Helkai; **16** Of Iddo, Zechariah; of Ginnethon, Meshullam; **17** Of Abijah, Zichri; of Miniamin, of Moadiah, Piltai; **18** Of Bilgah, Shammua; of Shemaiah, Jehonathan; **19** And of Joiarib, Mattenai; of Jedaiah, Uzzi; **20** Of Sallai, Kallai; of Amok, Eber; **21** Of Hilkiah, Hashabiah; of Jedaiah, Nethaneel. **22** The Levites in the days of Eliashib, Joiada, and Johanan, and Jaddua, were recorded chief of the fathers: also the priests, to the reign of Darius the Persian. **23** The sons of Levi, the chief of the fathers, were written in the book of the chronicles, even until the days of Johanan the son of Eliashib. **24** And the chief of the Levites: Hashabiah, Sherebiah, and Jeshua the son of Kadmiel, with their brethren over against them, to praise and to give thanks, *according to the commandment of David the man of God, ward over against ward.* **25** *Mattaniah, and Bakbukiah, Obadiah, Meshullam, Talmon, Akkub, were porters keeping the ward at the thresholds of the gates.* **26** *These were in the days of Joiakim the son of Jeshua, the son of Jozadak, and in the days of Nehemiah the governor, and of Ezra the priest, the scribe.* **27** *And at the dedication of the wall of Jerusalem they sought the Levites out of all their places, to bring them to Jerusalem, to keep the dedication with gladness, both with thanksgivings, and with singing, with cymbals, psalteries, and with harps.* **28** *And the sons of the singers gathered themselves together, both out of the plain country round about Jerusalem, and from the villages of Netophathi;* **29** *Also from the house of Gilgal, and out of the fields of Geba and Azmaveth: for the singers had builded them villages round about Jerusalem.* **30** *And the priests and the Levites purified themselves, and purified the people, and the gates, and the wall.* **31** *Then I brought up the princes of Judah upon the wall, and appointed two great companies of them that gave thanks, whereof one went on the right hand upon the wall toward the dung gate:* **32** *And after them went Hoshaiah, and half of the princes of Judah,* **33** *And Azariah, Ezra, and Meshullam,* **34** *Judah, and Benjamin, and Shemaiah, and Jeremiah,* **35** *And certain of the priests' sons with trumpets; namely, Zechariah the son of Jonathan, the son of Shemaiah, the son of Mattaniah, the son of Michaiah, the son of Zaccur, the son of Asaph:* **36** *And his brethren, Shemaiah, and Azarael, Milalai, Gilalai, Maai, Nethaneel, and Judah, Hanani, with the musical instruments of David the man of God, and Ezra the scribe before them.* **37** *And at the fountain gate, which was over against them, they went up by the stairs of the city of David, at the going up of the wall, above the house of David, even unto the water gate eastward.* **38** *And the other company of them that gave thanks went over against them, and I after them, and the half of the people upon the wall, from beyond the tower of the furnaces even unto the broad wall;* **39** *And from above the gate of Ephraim, and above the old gate, and above the fish gate, and the tower of Hananeel, and the tower of Meah, even unto the sheep gate: and they stood still in the prison gate.* **40** *So stood the two companies of them that gave thanks in the house of God,* and I, and the half of the rulers with me: **41** *And the priests; Eliakim, Maaseiah, Miniamin, Michaiah, Elioenai, Zechariah, and Hananiah, with trumpets;* **42** *And Maaseiah, and Shemaiah, and Eleazar, and Uzzi, and Jehohanan, and Malchijah, and Elam, and Ezer. And the singers sang loud, with Jezrahiah their overseer.* **43** *Also that day they offered great sacrifices, and rejoiced: for God had made them rejoice with great joy: the wives also and the children rejoiced: so that the joy of Jerusalem was heard even afar off.* **44** *And at that time were some appointed over the chambers for the treasures, for the offerings, for the firstfruits, and for the tithes, to gather into them out of the fields of the cities the portions of the law for the priests and Levites: for Judah rejoiced for the priests and for the Levites that waited.* **45** *And both the singers and the porters kept the ward of their God, and the ward of the purification, according to the commandment of David, and of Solomon his son.* **46** *For in the days of David and Asaph of old there were chief of the singers, and songs of praise and thanksgiving unto God.* **47** *And all Israel in the days of Zerubbabel, and in the days of Nehemiah, gave the portions of the singers and the porters, every day his portion: and they sanctified holy things unto the Levites; and the Levites sanctified them unto the children of Aaron.*

Here is a recap of what we have seen thus far in the book of Nehemiah:

In chapter one God moved on the heart of a man with a comfortable life and a comfortable job, a Jew by the name of Nehemiah. Nehemiah became burdened to rebuild the ravaged walls of Jerusalem. So in chapter two, after four months of praying, God had the king notice Nehemiah's sad countenance and ask him what was wrong. Nehemiah ended up being granted permission to go back and rebuild the walls and was also granted the material from the king's forests to do so.

But it was also in chapter two that enemies reared their heads. Chapter two verse ten says:

Nehemiah 2:10 *When Sanballat the Horonite, and Tobiah the servant, the Ammonite, heard of it, it grieved them exceedingly that there was come a man to seek the welfare of the children of Israel.*

115

It has always grieved the devil and his crowd whenever anyone seeks the welfare of the children of Israel.

When Nehemiah arrived, he did a secret, night-time inspection of the city to see what needed to be done. Then he told the rulers of the city what he had in mind, and they readily agreed to do the job. At that point a third enemy joined in with Sanballat and Tobiah, a man named Geshem. Undaunted, Nehemiah told them to back off, and that he was going to see the walls rebuilt.

In chapter three we read a detailed account of the people who engaged in the building, and of the gates and portions of the wall that they built.

In chapter four we found that the people had a mind to work, even if it meant holding a weapon in one hand and a tool in the other. By the time chapter four was done the wall was joined together all the way around and was at half of its intended height.

In chapter five Nehemiah had to take time to deal with internal problems. These people who had come back out of bondage were enslaving each other. They were charging each other insanely high interest on loans, they were treating each other like the heathens had treated them. Nehemiah led the way in showing everyone how to treat everyone else like they were supposed to.

In chapter six our attention was once again brought back to the enemies from without. This time they were much more subtle than before. What they could not accomplish by threats they tried to accomplish with trickery. Nehemiah did not fall for any of their tricks for even a moment.

Chapter seven was a long chapter, seventy-three verses, and in it Nehemiah took a genealogy and census of the people.

Chapter eight was all about an eight day revival. The people came to a city-wide preaching meeting and found that they were supposed to be keeping the Feast of Tabernacles. A day of weeping turned into the happiest of holidays. God's timing was perfect, and He knew His hard-working people needed to rejoice for a while.

Chapter nine was that in which we saw the people standing up and blessing the Lord, praising Him right out loud.

We also saw that they had a bunch of very good reasons to do so and that we do as well!

At the end of chapter nine, the very last verse, we read this:

Nehemiah 9:38 *And because of all this we make a sure covenant, and write it; and our princes, Levites, and priests, seal unto it.*

They made decisions on how they would behave, they put it in covenant, contract form, they wrote it out, and they signed their names to it. Chapter ten gave the details of who signed it and what was in it.

That brings us to an interesting point in the book of Nehemiah. The building is done, the dedicatory revival service is over, and things are off and rolling. The people find that there is regular, everyday work to do once the building project is completed. We will cover chapters eleven and twelve together, and I call this chapter "The Business that Follows the Building."

The Business of Occupying in a New Work

Nehemiah 11:1 *And the rulers of the people dwelt at Jerusalem: the rest of the people also cast lots, to bring one of ten to dwell in Jerusalem the holy city, and nine parts to dwell in other cities.*

There is an old saying, "My how things change!" Concerning Jerusalem today, thinking of the Jews and Muslims, do they all want to be there and have possession of it, or not? Yes! Seemingly every Jew on the planet, and most of the Muslims, want to be there. They want to occupy it, they dig in like ticks and refuse to leave under any circumstances. Jerusalem is the most hotly contested piece of property on the entire planet. And as you get into verse one, it may seem like that is the case in Nehemiah's day. They are casting lots to see which one tenth of the people will live in Jerusalem. But then you get to verse two, and the picture changes:

Nehemiah 11:2 *And the people blessed all the men, that willingly offered themselves to dwell at Jerusalem.*

They were not drawing lots to see who "got" to dwell in Jerusalem; they were drawing lots to see who "had" to dwell in Jerusalem! And those who stepped up and actually volunteered to do so were praised as heroes by the rest of the people! Jerusalem was still very much a city on the brink, with little or nothing to offer. They had a wall and a house of worship, and that was about it.

Thank God for people who volunteer to occupy in a new work!

Nehemiah 11:3 *Now these* **(these who volunteered and were chosen by lot to live there)** *are the chief of the province that dwelt in Jerusalem: but in the cities of Judah dwelt every one in his possession in their cities, to wit, Israel, the priests, and the Levites, and the Nethinims, and the children of Solomon's servants.*

Most of the people when they came back from captivity went to live where their families had formerly lived, including the list of those at the end of verse three. Verse four begins a list of some of the people who chose to live in Jerusalem, those who chose to occupy in a new work:

Nehemiah 11:4 *And at Jerusalem dwelt certain of the children of Judah, and of the children of Benjamin. Of the children of Judah; Athaiah the son of Uzziah, the son of Zechariah, the son of Amariah, the son of Shephatiah, the son of Mahalaleel, of the children of Perez; 5 And Maaseiah the son of Baruch, the son of Colhozeh, the son of Hazaiah, the son of Adaiah, the son of Joiarib, the son of Zechariah, the son of Shiloni. 6 All the sons of Perez that dwelt at Jerusalem were four hundred threescore and eight valiant men.*

Perez, also called Pharez, had 468 of his descendants living in the city, all accounted as valiant, brave men. Thank God for those who produce some brave boys in today's soft world!

Nehemiah 11:7 *And these are the sons of Benjamin; Sallu the son of Meshullam, the son of Joed, the son of Pedaiah, the son of Kolaiah, the son of Maaseiah, the son of Ithiel, the son of Jesaiah. 8 And after him Gabbai, Sallai, nine hundred twenty and eight. 9 And Joel the son of Zichri was their overseer: and Judah the son of Senuah was second over the city.*

Judah is an interesting case to me. Joel was the big dog, the man in charge over that section. Judah was the "second," meaning the assistant, the second man. That is a hard position.

118

Very few fulfill it right; the ones who do are priceless and precious.

Nehemiah 11:10 *Of the priests: Jedaiah the son of Joiarib, Jachin.* **11** *Seraiah the son of Hilkiah, the son of Meshullam, the son of Zadok, the son of Meraioth, the son of Ahitub, was the ruler of the house of God.* **12** *And their brethren that did the work of the house were eight hundred twenty and two: and Adaiah the son of Jeroham, the son of Pelaliah, the son of Amzi, the son of Zechariah, the son of Pashur, the son of Malchiah,* **13** *And his brethren, chief of the fathers, two hundred forty and two: and Amashai the son of Azareel, the son of Ahasai, the son of Meshillemoth, the son of Immer,* **14** *And their brethren, mighty men of valour, an hundred twenty and eight: and their overseer was Zabdiel, the son of one of the great men.*

Seraiah is described as the ruler of the house of God. That was the title given to the assistant of the high priest, the man who took care of all of the "stuff" (grass cutting, window washing) sort of like a proper, biblical deacon. He was a servant, a "ruler over service."

Three different groups of priestly servants are mentioned; a group of 822, a group of 242, and a group of 128. Their direct overseer, sort of like a supervisor, was a man named Zabdiel.

Nehemiah 11:15 *Also of the Levites: Shemaiah the son of Hashub, the son of Azrikam, the son of Hashabiah, the son of Bunni;* **16** *And Shabbethai and Jozabad, of the chief of the Levites, had the oversight of the outward business of the house of God.*

These were the people that interacted with others outside the house of God on business matters, for instance, buying materials, ordering flowers, etc.

Before we go too far, let me remind you that this does not bear much resemblance to the local church, and for good reason. This was the center of worship for the entire nation! If there was only one church in our entire nation and everyone went to it, it would need to be like this as well. But what is utterly foolish is to find a church of 80 people with this type of structure: fifteen committees, seven boards, and a 300 page constitution!

Nehemiah 11:17 *And Mattaniah the son of Micha, the son of Zabdi, the son of Asaph, was the principal to begin the thanksgiving in prayer: and Bakbukiah the second among his brethren, and Abda the son of Shammua, the son of Galal, the son of Jeduthun.* **18** *All the Levites in the holy city were two hundred fourscore and four.*

Mattaniah was what we would call the choir leader. He opened the service with "thanksgiving in prayer" which was a designation for a psalm of praise.

Nehemiah 11:19 *Moreover the porters, Akkub, Talmon, and their brethren that kept the gates, were an hundred seventy and two.*

The porters were the gatekeepers, the door openers and the security guys.

Nehemiah 11:20 *And the residue of Israel, of the priests, and the Levites, were in all the cities of Judah, every one in his inheritance.* **21** *But the Nethinims dwelt in Ophel: and Ziha and Gispa were over the Nethinims.*

The Nethinims are mentioned eight times in Nehemiah, seven times in Ezra (who was right there alongside Nehemiah) and once in I Chronicles 9:2. They are mentioned nowhere else in the Bible. They were the basest of temple servants, the wood hewers and water drawers, and in later years they became a butt of jokes, and their name itself became an insult. These are the men we observed earlier dwelling, but not working.

Nehemiah 11:22 *The overseer also of the Levites at Jerusalem was Uzzi the son of Bani, the son of Hashabiah, the son of Mattaniah, the son of Micha. Of the sons of Asaph, the singers were over the business of the house of God.* **23** *For it was the king's commandment concerning them, that a certain portion should be for the singers, due for every day.*

Here we have Uzzi mentioned as the overseer of the Levites at Jerusalem. That word means "inspector." A good reminder: you do not get what you *expect*, you get what you *inspect*! Then we have the sons of Asaph, the singers mentioned. You see Asaph and his sons mentioned throughout the Psalms. Singing has always been a part of worship that God expects and enjoys!

What I find amazing in this verse is that a heathen king realized how important this was. Artaxerxes appointed a salary for them! We obviously cannot do that in churches today; none of us have a king's wealth. But we should pay plenty of attention to having *the most spiritual people we have* produce the best music that they can produce.

I emphasize that because if it is otherwise, we have a *performance* instead of an *offering*...

Nehemiah 11:24 *And Pethahiah the son of Meshezabeel, of the children of Zerah the son of Judah, was at the king's hand in all matters concerning the people.*

This was the king's legal/civil council, the "go-between" between the king and the people.

Nehemiah 11:25 *And for the villages, with their fields, some of the children of Judah dwelt at Kirjatharba, and in the villages thereof, and at Dibon, and in the villages thereof, and at Jekabzeel, and in the villages thereof, 26 And at Jeshua, and at Moladah, and at Bethphelet, 27 And at Hazarshual, and at Beersheba, and in the villages thereof, 28 And at Ziklag, and at Mekonah, and in the villages thereof, 29 And at Enrimmon, and at Zareah, and at Jarmuth, 30 Zanoah, Adullam, and in their villages, at Lachish, and the fields thereof, at Azekah, and in the villages thereof. And they dwelt from Beersheba unto the valley of Hinnom. 31 The children also of Benjamin from Geba dwelt at Michmash, and Aija, and Bethel, and in their villages, 32 And at Anathoth, Nob, Ananiah, 33 Hazor, Ramah, Gittaim, 34 Hadid, Zeboim, Neballat, 35 Lod, and Ono, the valley of craftsmen. 36 And of the Levites were divisions in Judah, and in Benjamin.*

This is a general list of the population and the other places that they lived besides Jerusalem.

The Business of Praise, Worship, and Thanksgiving

Nehemiah 12:1 *Now these are the priests and the Levites that went up with Zerubbabel the son of Shealtiel, and Jeshua: Seraiah, Jeremiah, Ezra, 2 Amariah, Malluch, Hattush, 3 Shechaniah, Rehum, Meremoth, 4 Iddo, Ginnetho, Abijah, 5 Miamin, Maadiah, Bilgah, 6 Shemaiah, and Joiarib, Jedaiah, 7*

Sallu, Amok, Hilkiah, Jedaiah. These were the chief of the priests and of their brethren in the days of Jeshua.

These verses tell us the main priests that came from Babylon back to Jerusalem many years previous under Zerubbabel, Ezra being included among them. Walls are of no use unless God be worshiped, and thus God's men are mentioned.

Nehemiah 12:8 *Moreover the Levites: Jeshua, Binnui, Kadmiel, Sherebiah, Judah, and Mattaniah, which was over the thanksgiving* **(this was mentioned in the last chapter),** *he and his brethren.* **9** *Also Bakbukiah and Unni, their brethren, were over against them in the watches.*

Where the group from verse eight stood, the group from verse nine stood across from them.

Nehemiah 12:10 *And Jeshua begat Joiakim, Joiakim also begat Eliashib, and Eliashib begat Joiada,* **11** *And Joiada begat Jonathan, and Jonathan begat Jaddua.* **12** *And in the days of Joiakim were priests, the chief of the fathers: of Seraiah, Meraiah; of Jeremiah, Hananiah;* **13** *Of Ezra, Meshullam; of Amariah, Jehohanan;* **14** *Of Melicu, Jonathan; of Shebaniah, Joseph;* **15** *Of Harim, Adna; of Meraioth, Helkai;* **16** *Of Iddo, Zechariah; of Ginnethon, Meshullam;* **17** *Of Abijah, Zichri; of Miniamin, of Moadiah, Piltai;* **18** *Of Bilgah, Shammua; of Shemaiah, Jehonathan;* **19** *And of Joiarib, Mattenai; of Jedaiah, Uzzi;* **20** *Of Sallai, Kallai; of Amok, Eber;* **21** *Of Hilkiah, Hashabiah; of Jedaiah, Nethaneel.*

These verses show the succession of the high priests. This was extremely important for two reasons. One, it established their purity of descent, ensuring that they were actually qualified by genealogy to be serving in that capacity. Two, from this point onward, since they had no king, their chronology would be reckoned by the succession of their priests.[2]

Nehemiah 12:22 *The Levites in the days of Eliashib, Joiada, and Johanan, and Jaddua, were recorded chief of the fathers: also the priests, to the reign of Darius the Persian.* **23** *The sons of Levi, the chief of the fathers, were written in the book of the chronicles, even until the days of Johanan the son of Eliashib.*

This is not the books of Chronicles we have in the Bible; no such list is found there. There were many other "books of Chronicles."

Nehemiah 12:24 *And the chief of the Levites: Hashabiah, Sherebiah, and Jeshua the son of Kadmiel, with their brethren over against them, to praise and to give thanks, according to the commandment of David the man of God, ward over against ward.* **25** *Mattaniah, and Bakbukiah, Obadiah, Meshullam, Talmon, Akkub, were porters keeping the ward at the thresholds of the gates.* **26** *These were in the days of Joiakim the son of Jeshua, the son of Jozadak, and in the days of Nehemiah the governor, and of Ezra the priest, the scribe.*

In verse twenty-four you once again see people facing each other, with the purpose of praising God. We will see a very full description of this in just a few verses. But for now just notice that these particular people did this for a lot of years, during the times of Joiakim, Nehemiah, and Ezra.

Nehemiah 12:27 *And at the dedication of the wall of Jerusalem they sought the Levites out of all their places, to bring them to Jerusalem, to keep the dedication with gladness, both with thanksgivings, and with singing, with cymbals, psalteries, and with harps.* **28** *And the sons of the singers gathered themselves together, both out of the plain country round about Jerusalem, and from the villages of Netophathi;* **29** *Also from the house of Gilgal, and out of the fields of Geba and Azmaveth: for the singers had builded them villages round about Jerusalem.* **30** *And the priests and the Levites purified themselves, and purified the people, and the gates, and the wall.* **31** *Then I brought up the princes of Judah upon the wall, and appointed two great companies of them that gave thanks, whereof one went on the right hand upon the wall toward the dung gate:* **32** *And after them went Hoshaiah, and half of the princes of Judah,* **33** *And Azariah, Ezra, and Meshullam,* **34** *Judah, and Benjamin, and Shemaiah, and Jeremiah,* **35** *And certain of the priests' sons with trumpets; namely, Zechariah the son of Jonathan, the son of Shemaiah, the son of Mattaniah, the son of Michaiah, the son of Zaccur, the son of Asaph:* **36** *And his brethren, Shemaiah, and Azarael, Milalai, Gilalai, Maai, Nethaneel, and Judah, Hanani, with the musical instruments of David the man of God, and Ezra* *the scribe before them. 37 And at the fountain gate, which was over against them, they went up by the stairs of the city of David, at the going up of the wall, above the house of David, even unto the water gate eastward. 38 And the other company of them that gave thanks went over against them, and I after them, and the half of the people upon the wall, from beyond the tower of the furnaces even unto the broad wall; 39 And from above the gate of Ephraim, and above the old gate, and above the fish gate, and the tower of Hananeel, and the tower of Meah, even unto the sheep gate: and they stood still in the prison gate. 40 So stood the two companies of them that gave thanks in the house of God, and I, and the half of the rulers with me: 41 And the priests; Eliakim, Maaseiah, Miniamin, Michaiah, Elioenai, Zechariah, and Hananiah, with trumpets; 42 And Maaseiah, and Shemaiah, and Eleazar, and Uzzi, and Jehohanan, and Malchijah, and Elam, and Ezer. And the singers sang loud, with Jezrahiah their overseer. 43 Also that day they offered great sacrifices, and rejoiced: for God had made them rejoice with great joy: the wives also and the children rejoiced: so that the joy of Jerusalem was heard even afar off. 44 And at that time were some appointed over the chambers for the treasures, for the offerings, for the firstfruits, and for the tithes, to gather into them out of the fields of the cities the portions of the law for the priests and Levites: for Judah rejoiced for the priests and for the Levites that waited. 45 And both the singers and the porters kept the ward of their God, and the ward of the purification, according to the commandment of David, and of Solomon his son. 46 For in the days of David and Asaph of old there were chief of the singers, and songs of praise and thanksgiving unto God. 47 And all Israel in the days of Zerubbabel, and in the days of Nehemiah, gave the portions of the singers and the porters, every day his portion: and they sanctified holy things unto the Levites; and the Levites sanctified them unto the children of Aaron.*

The very first thing we notice is that the people were divided into two great companies. The second thing you see is that instead of standing in the middle of it all, they made their way up onto the wall. The third thing we see is that they went two different directions and encircled the entire city. That was their way of indicating that they ought to be giving thanks for everything. They believed that God brought them every single thing that they were, at that moment, so grateful for.

Everything in your life that you prize so dearly is a gift from God!

After they had the circle formed, they were not only looking out at all that God had done, they were also looking across the way at someone on the other side. That is what made the next part so significant. When they began to give thanks, there was somebody over there that they were directing it to. The next thing you see is that they did not just speak thanksgiving, they then sang thanksgiving:

God is so good, God is so good, God is so good, He's so good to me...

As the world looks upon me, as I struggle along, and they say I have nothing but they are so wrong, in my heart I'm rejoicing, how I wish they could see. Thank you Lord, for your blessings on me! I've a roof up above me and a good place to sleep, there is food on my table, and shoes on my feet. You gave me your love Lord, and a fine family, thank you Lord for your blessings on me.

Chapter Twelve
Out with the Ammonites

Nehemiah 13:1 *On that day they read in the book of Moses in the audience of the people; and therein was found written, that the Ammonite and the Moabite should not come into the congregation of God for ever;* **2** *Because they met not the children of Israel with bread and with water, but hired Balaam against them, that he should curse them: howbeit our God turned the curse into a blessing.* **3** *Now it came to pass, when they had heard the law, that they separated from Israel all the mixed multitude.* **4** *And before this, Eliashib the priest, having the oversight of the chamber of the house of our God, was allied unto Tobiah:* **5** *And he had prepared for him a great chamber, where aforetime they laid the meat offerings, the frankincense, and the vessels, and the tithes of the corn, the new wine, and the oil, which was commanded to be given to the Levites, and the singers, and the porters; and the offerings of the priests.* **6** *But in all this time was not I at Jerusalem: for in the two and thirtieth year of Artaxerxes king of Babylon came I unto the king, and after certain days obtained I leave of the king:* **7** *And I came to Jerusalem, and understood of the evil that Eliashib did for Tobiah, in preparing him a chamber in the courts of the house of God.* **8** *And it grieved me sore: therefore I cast forth all the household stuff of Tobiah out of the chamber.* **9** *Then I commanded, and they cleansed the chambers: and thither brought I again the vessels of the house of God, with the meat* *offering and the frankincense.* **10** *And I perceived that the portions of the Levites had not been given them: for the Levites and the singers, that did the work, were fled every one to his field.* **11** *Then contended I with the rulers, and said, Why is the house of God forsaken? And I gathered them together, and set them in their place.* **12** *Then brought all Judah the tithe of the corn and the new wine and the oil unto the treasuries.* **13** *And I made treasurers over the treasuries, Shelemiah the priest, and Zadok the scribe, and of the Levites, Pedaiah: and next to them was Hanan the son of Zaccur, the son of Mattaniah: for they were counted faithful, and their office was to distribute unto their brethren.* **14** *Remember me, O my God, concerning this, and wipe not out my good deeds that I have done for the house of my God, and for the offices thereof.* **15** *In those days saw I in Judah some treading wine presses on the sabbath, and bringing in sheaves, and lading asses; as also wine, grapes, and figs, and all manner of burdens, which they brought into Jerusalem on the sabbath day: and I testified against them in the day wherein they sold victuals.* **16** *There dwelt men of Tyre also therein, which brought fish, and all manner of ware, and sold on the sabbath unto the children of Judah, and in Jerusalem.* **17** *Then I contended with the nobles of Judah, and said unto them, What evil thing is this that ye do, and profane the sabbath day?* **18** *Did not your fathers thus, and did not our God bring all this evil upon us, and upon this city? yet ye bring more wrath upon Israel by profaning the sabbath.* **19** *And it came to pass, that when the gates of Jerusalem began to be dark before the sabbath, I commanded that the gates should be shut, and charged that they should not be opened till after the sabbath: and some of my servants set I at the gates, that there should no burden be brought in on the sabbath day.* **20** *So the merchants and sellers of all kind of ware lodged without Jerusalem once or twice.* **21** *Then I testified against them, and said unto them, Why lodge ye about the wall? if ye do so again, I will lay hands on you. From that time forth came they no more on the sabbath.* **22** *And I commanded the Levites that they should cleanse themselves, and that they should come and keep the gates, to sanctify the sabbath day. Remember me, O my God, concerning this also, and spare me according to the greatness of thy mercy.* **23** *In those days* *also saw I Jews that had married wives of Ashdod, of Ammon, and of Moab:* **24** *And their children spake half in the speech of Ashdod, and could not speak in the Jews' language, but according to the language of each people.* **25** *And I contended with them, and cursed them, and smote certain of them, and plucked off their hair, and made them swear by God, saying, Ye shall not give your daughters unto their sons, nor take their daughters unto your sons, or for yourselves.* **26** *Did not Solomon king of Israel sin by these things? yet among many nations was there no king like him, who was beloved of his God, and God made him king over all Israel: nevertheless even him did outlandish women cause to sin.* **27** *Shall we then hearken unto you to do all this great evil, to transgress against our God in marrying strange wives?* **28** *And one of the sons of Joiada, the son of Eliashib the high priest, was son in law to Sanballat the Horonite: therefore I chased him from me.* **29** *Remember them, O my God, because they have defiled the priesthood, and the covenant of the priesthood, and of the Levites.* **30** *Thus cleansed I them from all strangers, and appointed the wards of the priests and the Levites, every one in his business;* **31** *And for the wood offering, at times appointed, and for the firstfruits. Remember me, O my God, for good.*

Things had come so very far since God placed a burden upon one man's heart to go and rebuild the walls of Jerusalem. Nehemiah had come from Persia, set to the task, rallied the people, defended the work against enemies within and without, called for a revival, and accomplished all that he set his hand to do. The walls were now built, the city was fully functioning, but there was still no place for complacency and ease. A new problem was discovered in this very last chapter, and it would have to be dealt with. Ammonites, those inveterate foes of Israel, had been allowed into the midst. When enemies are allowed into the midst of a country, a home, or a church, disaster is sure to follow. What happens when "Ammonites" are allowed in the midst?

God's House Is Corrupted

Nehemiah 13:1 *On that day they read in the book of Moses in the audience of the people; and therein was found written, that the Ammonite and the Moabite should not come into the congregation of God for ever;* **2** *Because they met not the children of Israel with bread and with water, but hired Balaam against them, that he should curse them: howbeit our God turned the curse into a blessing.*

"That day" does not refer to the day of the dedication of the wall. As you will see from later verses in the chapter it refers to a day when Nehemiah, after having been gone back to the palace in Persia for a while, returned to see how things were going.[3] [4]

On that day, whenever it was, the Pentateuch was again read before the people. When it was, they read this:

Deuteronomy 23:3 *An Ammonite or Moabite shall not enter into the congregation of the LORD; even to their tenth generation shall they not enter into the congregation of the LORD for ever:* **4** *Because they met you not with bread and with water in the way, when ye came forth out of Egypt; and because they hired against thee Balaam the son of Beor of Pethor of Mesopotamia, to curse thee.*

God knew that the Ammonites and Moabites were the inveterate enemies of Israel and were not going to change. The few examples of those that got saved, like Ruth, ceased to be Moabites or Ammonites and became proselytes to Judaism. God commanded in no uncertain terms that they, especially the Ammonites, not be allowed to infect God's people with their filthy ways and ideas.

Nehemiah 13:3 *Now it came to pass, when they had heard the law, that they separated from Israel all the mixed multitude.*

The people had already failed miserably in observing God's law on this matter. By the time Nehemiah got back, there were already a great number of the people who were tied in with these heathens. To their credit, once they realized their error, they corrected it. People like that are incredibly rare! Normally, when people have their faults pointed out, they respond by either justifying their behavior or lashing out at those who pointed out their errors.

Why is it so dangerous to allow Ammonites (heathens, non-believers who want the benefits of God's people and God's house) into our lives? Because it will corrupt God's house.

Nehemiah 13:4 *And before this, Eliashib the priest, having the oversight of the chamber of the house of our God, was allied unto Tobiah: 5 And he had prepared for him a great chamber, where aforetime they laid the meat offerings, the frankincense, and the vessels, and the tithes of the corn, the new wine, and the oil, which was commanded to be given to the Levites, and the singers, and the porters; and the offerings of the priests.*

There is an amazing and saddening turn in this verse. It is obvious that Eliashib is doing something very wrong, and we will get to his deed in a moment. But I first want to remind you who he was:

Nehemiah 3:1 *Then Eliashib the high priest rose up with his brethren the priests, and they builded the sheep gate; they sanctified it, and set up the doors of it; even unto the tower of Meah they sanctified it, unto the tower of Hananeel.*

This man was not just "a" priest, he was the high priest, and he was one of the builders of the wall, having worked on the Sheep Gate. Just because you began well in your walk with God does not mean you will finish well. If you begin to court the wrong crowd, your end will be bad enough to wipe away the memory of your beginning.

What did he do? He made an elaborate place in the temple, a luxury apartment, a "great chamber" for Tobiah to live in. This used to be the place where the offerings were stored. You doubtless remember that Tobiah was one of the main enemies of Nehemiah and the wall builders! Throughout the book, he fought against everything God's people were doing. But do you remember *what* he was?

Nehemiah 4:3 *Now Tobiah the Ammonite was by him, and he said, Even that which they build, if a fox go up, he shall even break down their stone wall.*

131

Tobiah, the mocking, snotty, attitudinal guy, was an Ammonite. They made a nice place in the temple for this Ammonite to come and live!

Not everyone needs to be allowed into our churches. People who repent, trust Christ, are not harmful, and agree to follow the leading of God's Word and God's man should be allowed. But there are people who are not saved, do not want to be saved, do not follow God's Word, do not want to follow God's Word, will not follow God's man, do not want to follow God's man, yet still want to be a part of the church. They like the social status it affords, they like the opportunities to be placed in a position of prominence, they like the social interaction, but they do nothing but cause problems for God's man and whatever church people want to live right. They are Ammonites and ought not to be allowed back inside the doors!

Nehemiah 13:6 *But in all this time was not I at Jerusalem: for in the two and thirtieth year of Artaxerxes king of Babylon came I unto the king, and after certain days obtained I leave of the king: 7 And I came to Jerusalem, and understood of the evil that Eliashib did for Tobiah, in preparing him a chamber in the courts of the house of God.*

"Nehemiah came to Jerusalem in the twentieth year of Artaxerxes, and remained there till the thirty-second year, twelve years: then returned to Babylon, and stayed one year; got leave to revisit his brethren; and found matters as stated in this chapter."[5]

Nehemiah was not happy, not happy at all. All of the work he did, and within a year of being gone, a foolish priest was letting an Ammonite live in the temple! But Nehemiah was a man who knew how to "tactfully handle" such a delicate situation:

Nehemiah 13:8 *And it grieved me sore: therefore I cast forth all the household stuff of Tobiah out of the chamber.*

That is positively hilarious! Nehemiah literally threw all of the guy's stuff out to the curb! Can you just imagine the conversation between him and the more "diplomatic" members of the congregation?

"Um, now, uh, Nehemiah, I understand that you are a wee bit upset about the Ammonite in the temple. But I want you

132

to remember, this is God's house, and everyone is welcome here, even if they are here to cause trouble..."

Crash, bang, clank clank clank clank!

"Now, Nehemiah, you really shouldn't do that. It might hurt Tobiah's feelings if you keep throwing his stuff out, and the most important thing in the world is to make sure that we don't hurt anyone's feelings..."

Heave! Whoosh, bang bang bang bang bang!

"Now really, preacher, don't you think that everybody needs to be in God's house, even if they are having a terrible influence on those around them?"

Uggggggggh! Boom boom boom boom boom...

I would love for Nehemiah to be a pastor serving today, near to my church. For once, people would think that I am a pretty patient guy!

Let me say something. "Everyone welcome" should not really be the motto of our churches. I understand what people are trying to say. "Whatever your race, gender, socio-economic status, you are welcome here." I get that, and I agree with it. But we have had to do church discipline twice at our church, and those people are not welcome until they repent.

There is a fifty-some year old pervert in our area. A few years ago, he decided to chat online with a fourteen year old girl and solicit her for sex. When he met her at the local mall, the fourteen year old girl turned out to be a local police officer. Welcome the guy at your church if you like, but with as many teenage girls as we have in ours, he is not welcome at mine.

We had a guy cause us a ton of trouble, demanding to be put in charge of the finances. If he is welcome at your church, let me know, I'll track him down and put him in touch with you. But I do not need that kind of a headache.

A church is an *ekklesia*; a "called out assembly". By definition, we are not "all inclusive." People who repent, trust Christ, are not harmful, and agree to follow the leading of God's Word and God's man should be allowed.

When Ammonites are let in, God's house is corrupted.

God's Men Are Cut

Nehemiah 13:9 *Then I commanded, and they cleansed the chambers: and thither brought I again the vessels of the house of God, with the meat offering and the frankincense.* **10** *And I perceived that the portions of the Levites had not been given them: for the Levites and the singers, that did the work, were fled every one to his field.*

Nehemiah took time and "fumigated" the room Tobiah had been staying in. He converted it back into the temple storeroom for the offerings. It was then that it dawned on him that since Tobiah had been in the storeroom, there had been no offerings to pay the men of God. They had to go take secular work just to survive.

I have yet to see an exception to this. When you let "Ammonites" into the house of God, they eventually end up in positions of influence, and they always use that influence against God's man.

Nehemiah 13:11 *Then contended I with the rulers, and said, Why is the house of God forsaken? And I gathered them together, and set them in their place.*

Nehemiah, once more showing "incredible tact and diplomacy," chewed the rulers out! He *contended with them* and *set them in their place.*

Nehemiah 13:12 *Then brought all Judah the tithe of the corn and the new wine and the oil unto the treasuries.* **13** *And I made treasurers over the treasuries, Shelemiah the priest, and Zadok the scribe, and of the Levites, Pedaiah: and next to them was Hanan the son of Zaccur, the son of Mattaniah: for they were counted faithful, and their office was to distribute unto their brethren.* **14** *Remember me, O my God, concerning this, and wipe not out my good deeds that I have done for the house of my God, and for the offices thereof.*

Nehemiah removed the Ammonite, and shortly thereafter God's men were being taken care of again.

When Ammonites are let in, God's house is corrupted, and God's men are cut.

God's Day Is Cheapened

Nehemiah 13:15 *In those days saw I in Judah some treading wine presses on the sabbath, and bringing in sheaves, and lading asses; as also wine, grapes, and figs, and all manner of burdens, which they brought into Jerusalem on the sabbath day: and I testified against them in the day wherein they sold victuals.*

People seem to forget their promises so quickly:

Nehemiah 10:29 *They clave to their brethren, their nobles, and entered into a curse, and into an oath, to walk in God's law, which was given by Moses the servant of God, and to observe and do all the commandments of the LORD our Lord, and his judgments and his statutes;* **30** *And that we would not give our daughters unto the people of the land, nor take their daughters for our sons:* **31** *And if the people of the land bring ware or any victuals on the sabbath day to sell, that we would not buy it of them on the sabbath, or on the holy day: and that we would leave the seventh year, and the exaction of every debt.*

They promised! Yet just a short while later, here they are again. They allowed Ammonites in the midst, and the next thing you know, God's day was cheapened:

A pastor a few states away had an "Ammonitess" show up at his place. Some of his teens started missing church on Sunday, and when he started poking around and asking questions, he found that this girl was having "Christian activities" on those days and inviting his youth group to attend them with her. Oh no, that did not go over *well at all...*

Nehemiah 13:16 *There dwelt men of Tyre also therein, which brought fish, and all manner of ware, and sold on the sabbath unto the children of Judah, and in Jerusalem.* **17** *Then I contended with the nobles of Judah, and said unto them, What evil thing is this that ye do, and profane the sabbath day?* **18** *Did not your fathers thus, and did not our God bring all this evil upon us, and upon this city? yet ye bring more wrath upon Israel by profaning the sabbath.*

Nehemiah and his tact once more. He had the gall to point out that God was actually *angry* over how they were cheapening His day (Cough! Super Bowl parties instead of service.) I mean, he told them that they were wrong to be cheapening His day (Cough! Rock Bands in the sanctuary masquerading as "Christian Artists.) I mean, can you imagine the gall of Nehemiah, chewing them out for cheapening God's day (Cough! Casual service, dress to go to the lake just come on to church first.)...

Nehemiah 13:19 *And it came to pass, that when the gates of Jerusalem began to be dark before the sabbath, I commanded that the gates should be shut, and charged that they should not be opened till after the sabbath: and some of my servants set I at the gates, that there should no burden be brought in on the sabbath day.* **20** *So the merchants and sellers of all kind of ware lodged without Jerusalem once or twice.* **21** *Then I testified against them, and said unto them, Why lodge ye about the wall? if ye do so again, I will lay hands on you. From that time forth came they no more on the sabbath.*

I love this one. When they could not get into the city to set up their tables, they set them up just outside the walls, so people could come out and do business. They figured that was "outside of Nehemiah's jurisdiction." Nehemiah did not think so! He figured that if something outside the walls affected things inside the walls, it was, in fact, his business. Oh how preachers today are hated for taking that same position!

How dare you voice an opinion on who my child dates!

How dare you say that my Susie ought not to dress like a streetwalker at school!

How dare you correct my child for what she put on Facebook!

How dare you tell me not to sell beer in my store!

Nehemiah made it his business to the extent that he threatened to "lay hands on them" if they kept coming around!

Nehemiah 13:22 *And I commanded the Levites that they should cleanse themselves, and that they should come and keep the gates, to sanctify the sabbath day. Remember me, O my God, concerning this also, and spare me according to the greatness of thy mercy.*

Nehemiah enlisted the help of all of God's men to keep the Sabbath day pure.

When Ammonites are let in, God's house is corrupted, God's men are cut, and God's day is cheapened.

God's People Are Confused

Nehemiah 13:23 *In those days also saw I Jews that had married wives of Ashdod, of Ammon, and of Moab:* **24** *And their children spake half in the speech of Ashdod, and could not speak in the Jews' language, but according to the language of each people.*

Talk about confusing! These Jewish men made the same mistake as Solomon by marrying strange, foreign, unbelieving women. Those women raised the children speaking in the mother's native tongue. Half of the kids mentioned could speak the language of Ashdod, but none could speak Hebrew. This was not a "racist" thing for Nehemiah to confront this problem. It was not about skin; it was about sin. These kids could not understand Hebrew, meaning they could not be taught about the God of the Hebrews. Because they opened the door for Ammonites, everything else flooded in as well, and it resulted in spiritual confusion.

And if you think you have seen Nehemiah mad previously, trust me, you have not. When he found out that the sins of the adults were affecting his young people, he went ballistic:

Nehemiah 13:25 *And I contended with them, and cursed them* **(this does not mean he uttered profanities, it means he pronounced oaths of judgment against them)**, *and smote certain of them, and plucked off their hair, and made them swear by God, saying, Ye shall not give your daughters unto their sons, nor take their daughters unto your sons, or for yourselves.*

Nehemiah actually slapped them around and yanked out their hair! Repeat after me: "My pastor is a nice guy after all; my pastor is a nice guy after all..."

Nehemiah 13:26 *Did not Solomon king of Israel sin by these things? yet among many nations was there no king like him, who was beloved of his God, and God made him king over all Israel: nevertheless even him did outlandish women cause to sin.* **27** *Shall we then hearken unto you to do all this great evil, to transgress against our God in marrying strange wives?*

God has never changed His mind on this. It is always a sin for a believer to marry a non-believer. And do not think it

137

will not impact you negatively. If it impacted Solomon, it will impact you.

Nehemiah 13:28 *And one of the sons of Joiada, the son of Eliashib the high priest, was son in law to Sanballat the Horonite: therefore I chased him from me.*

Let me read you Adam Clarke's take on this verse, if for no other reason, just because of a word he uses, which, I have decided, is quite possibly the coolest word of all times:

> "Those who set at open defiance the laws of God and man, and whose continued presence is inconsistent with the welfare of the community, should not be permitted to live in it; and in all wise and good efforts to prevent their **pestiferous** influence, men may expect the aid of the enlightened, patriotic, and good, and the blessing of God."[6]

I love that. If a person's influence is going to be "pestiferous," they ought not to be allowed to continue among us.

Nehemiah 13:29 *Remember them, O my God, because they have defiled the priesthood, and the covenant of the priesthood, and of the Levites.* **30** *Thus cleansed I them from all strangers, and appointed the wards of the priests and the Levites, every one in his business;* **31** *And for the wood offering, at times appointed, and for the firstfruits. Remember me, O my God, for good.*

Nehemiah cleaned out the Ammonites and concluded by saying, *Remember me, O my God, for good.* He expected God to bless him for doing so, and he was right.

When Ammonites are let in, God's house is corrupted, God's men are cut, God's day is cheapened, and God's people are confused.

Out with the Ammonites!

Epilogue

The rubble is still about the burned and ruined walls. But in our day, the walls that have produced the rubble are the walls of the local church in America. Assaults from without and complacency from within have resulted in defenseless and ineffective bodies of believers. Yet the power of God has not changed nor has His desire. He is still seeking for a man, a man who will view the restoration of those walls as the only thing worth living for. Such a man (or woman or boy or girl...) can move mountains, overcome opposition, and produce walls from rubble.

Dear reader, vow to be that man...

Notes

1. The King James Study Bible, Nelson Publishers, introduction to the book of Nehemiah

2. Robert Jamison, A. R. Fausset, David Brown, *A Commentary of the Old and New Testament,* 3 vols. (Peabody, MA: Hendrickson Publishers, 2008) 1: 638

3. Adam Clarke, LL.D., F.S.A, &c., *Clarke's Commentary*, 6 vols. (New York: Abingdon-Cokesbury Press) 2:795

4. John Wesley Notes, *Power BibleCD* (Bronson, MI: Online Publishing, Inc., 2003) Nehemiah 13:1

5. Adam Clarke, LL.D., F.S.A, &c., *Clarke's Commentary*, 6 vols. (New York: Abingdon-Cokesbury Press) 2:795

6. Family Bible Notes, *Power BibleCD* (Bronson, MI: Online Publishing, Inc., 2003) Nehemiah 13:28

Made in the USA
Charleston, SC
04 November 2015